IMAGES OF WAR

OPERATION HÖSS

THE DEPORTATION OF HUNGARIAN JEWS TO AUSCHWITZ-BIRKENAU MAY–JULY 1944

RARE PHOTOGRAPHS FROM WARTIME ARCHIVES

Ian Baxter

Pen & Sword
MILITARY

First published in Great Britain in 2022 by
PEN & SWORD MILITARY
an imprint of Pen & Sword Books Ltd
Yorkshire – Philadelphia

Copyright © Ian Baxter, 2022

ISBN 978-1-39906-290-9

The right of Ian Baxter to be identified as the author of this work has been asserted by him in accordance with the Copyright, Designs and Patents Act 1988.

A CIP catalogue record for this book is available from the British Library.

All rights reserved. No part of this book may be reproduced or transmitted in any form or by any means, electronic or mechanical including photocopying, recording or by any information storage and retrieval system, without permission from the Publisher in writing.

Typeset by Concept, Huddersfield, West Yorkshire, HD4 5JL.
Printed and bound in England by CPI Group (UK) Ltd, Croydon CR0 4YY.

Pen & Sword Books Limited incorporates the imprints of Atlas, Archaeology, Aviation, Discovery, Family History, Fiction, History, Maritime, Military, Military Classics, Politics, Select, Transport, True Crime, Air World, Frontline Publishing, Leo Cooper, Remember When, Seaforth Publishing, The Praetorian Press, Wharncliffe Local History, Wharncliffe Transport, Wharncliffe True Crime and White Owl.

For a complete list of Pen & Sword titles please contact
PEN & SWORD BOOKS LTD
47 Church Street, Barnsley, South Yorkshire, S70 2AS, England
E-mail: enquiries@pen-and-sword.co.uk
Website: www.pen-and-sword.co.uk
or
PEN & SWORD BOOKS
1950 Lawrence Rd, Havertown, PA 19083, USA
E-mail: uspen-and-sword@casematepublishers.com
Website: www.penandswordbooks.com

Contents

Introduction **5**

Chapter One
Preparations **7**

Chapter Two
Deportation **17**

Chapter Three
Arrival **27**

Chapter Four
Slave Labour **69**

Chapter Five
Murder **83**

Chapter Six
The Aftermath **111**

Appendix One
Timeline **119**

Appendix Two
Hungarian Jewish Ghettos **123**

Appendix Three
Kassa List **125**

Appendix Four
Hungarians Deported and Selected for Labour **129**

Appendix Five
Detailed Listing of Male and Female Train Transports . **131**

About the Author

Ian Baxter is a military historian who specialises in German twentieth-century military history. He has written more than fifty books including *Poland – The Eighteen Day Victory March*, *Panzers In North Africa*, *The Ardennes Offensive*, *The Western Campaign*, *The 12th SS Panzer-Division Hitlerjugend*, *The Waffen-SS on the Western Front*, *The Waffen-SS on the Eastern Front*, *The Red Army at Stalingrad*, *Elite German Forces of World War II*, *Armoured Warfare*, *German Tanks of War*, *Blitzkrieg*, *Panzer-Divisions at War*, *Hitler's Panzers*, *German Armoured Vehicles of World War Two*, *Last Two Years of the Waffen-SS at War*, *German Soldier Uniforms and Insignia*, *German Guns of the Third Reich*, *Defeat to Retreat: The Last Years of the German Army At War 1943–45*, *Operation Bagration – the Destruction of Army Group Centre*, *German Guns of the Third Reich*, *Rommel and the Afrika Korps*, *U-Boat War*, and most recently *The Sixth Army and the Road to Stalingrad*. He has written over a hundred articles including 'Last days of Hitler', 'Wolf's Lair', 'The Story of the V1 and V2 Rocket Programme', 'Secret Aircraft of World War Two', 'Rommel at Tobruk', 'Hitler's War With his Generals', 'Secret British Plans to Assassinate Hitler', 'The SS at Arnhem', 'Hitlerjugend', 'Battle of Caen 1944', 'Gebirgsjäger at War', 'Panzer Crews', 'Hitlerjugend Guerrillas', 'Last Battles in the East', 'The Battle of Berlin', and many more. He has also reviewed numerous military studies for publication, supplied thousands of photographs and important documents to various publishers and film production companies worldwide, and lectures to various schools, colleges and universities throughout the United Kingdom and the Republic of Ireland.

Introduction

In May and June 1944, the Nazis deported more than 430,000 Jews from Hungary to Auschwitz-Birkenau. This was known by the SS as Operation HÖSS, named after the camp commander Rudolf Höss who was called back to oversee the action.

Many of the photographs in this book were taken by the *Politische Abteilung Erkennungsdienst* or the 'Political Department Identification Service'. The department also had a photographic service responsible for cataloguing inmates by taking photographs, which included portraits of registered prisoners that were not sent directly to the gas chambers. Images also included the gassing process, various experiments, escape attempts and suicides. The *Erkennungsdienst* was headed by Director *SS-Hauptscharführer* Bernhard Walter and Deputy Director Ernst Hofmann, but it was Bernhard Walter who took the majority of the images that became known as *Aussiedlung der Juden aus Ungarn* or *The Deportation of the Hungarian Jews*. The album comprised 56 pages and 193 photographs, which were later donated to Yad Vashem Holocaust Museum in Israel.

The purpose of the album is not clear, but one thing is apparent: the Nazis were obsessed with documentation. As a result the photographers wanted to catalogue the processing of the inmates at Birkenau: those that were to live and those that were destined to die. Various images show the inmates being unloaded from the cattle car trains onto the crowded ramps. Wilhelm Brasse, who was one of the political prisoners and had once worked in a photography studio in Katowice, was forced to take photos for the *Erkennungsdienst* using his Kodak Retina camera. He recalls that he developed and printed some of the photos for Walter for the album. Over a period of several days the various images showed the unloading of the Hungarian Jews from Carpathian Ruthenia and their selection at the ramp. The two photographers covered those people considered fit to work and those on their final walk.

During this time Walter and his number two Hofmann kept focusing their cameras on the women, children, the old and the infirm. The Jews looked worn, tired and perplexed, but Walter noted that they did not display any sign of fear. Both men followed groups of those selected for work and those selected for death to a birch grove just outside the crematoria, where they were made to wait before being killed.

Through the lens of the camera a series of images was taken in order to prove that in spite of their fate, there was still an air of calm. Many of the men, women and children in the woods stared directly at the camera while Walter and Hofmann snapped away taking photos of their last moments before they were led away and murdered. The photographers also documented the workings of the 'Kanada' storage facilities, where the looted belongings of the prisoners were sorted before transport to the Reich for the war effort.

The album's survival is remarkable given the arduous efforts made by the Nazis to keep the so-called 'Final Solution' a secret. Although the photographs in this book are unsettling, it is a unique document and the only surviving visual evidence of the process leading to the mass murder at Auschwitz-Birkenau.

* * *

The views or opinions expressed in this book and the content in which the images are used do not necessarily reflect the views or policy of or imply approval or endorsement by the United States Holocaust Memorial Museum (USHMM).

Chapter One

Preparations

The year 1944 opened up with a frustrating series of military setbacks for the German war machine. On the Eastern Front the Red Army had made considerable gains and was driving their disordered enemy back towards the frontiers of the Reich. The Nazi newspapers revealed how heroic German legions were fighting to the grim death and through the sacrifices of the fallen the German nation would emerge victorious, but throughout the Reich and indeed all over the occupied countries the picture was far bleaker than ever before. In order to stave off defeat, the need to increase armaments production had become such a major priority. The problem was so acute that it was considered there might even be a temporary change of policy towards the destruction of the Jews. Although those unfit for work would still be killed, the process of what the Nazis termed 'special treatment' could perhaps be more selective and mass killing counterproductive. With death camps like Kulmhof, Sobibor, Belzec and Treblinka now closed down, it was up to the other camps, in particular Auschwitz-Birkenau, which was to take responsibility for the remnants of the Jewish communities of Poland, France, the Netherlands, Italy and the rest of occupied Europe. Here more stringent selections would have to take place with many new arrivals being used for the German war industry.

Over the next weeks and months the Nazis undertook drastic measures to get as many prisoners as possible that were destined for the extermination camps to work in the armaments factories. Even Albert Speer, the Minister of Armaments, was particularly insistent that if Germany was to stave off defeat, then the armament factories needed to be replenished with increased labour. By the end of February 1944, the labour shortage was so bad that Hitler himself intervened, instructing *SS-Reichsführer* Heinrich Himmler to obtain 100,000 Jewish slave workers from the sole remaining Jewish community in Europe, Hungary.

For some time the German Foreign Office had been badgering the Hungarian government to toughen its anti-Jewish laws. Reports from *SS-Obersturmbannführer* Adolf Eichmann's office indicated that there were almost 725,000 Jews on Hungarian territory, and for the German government that figure was too great an opportunity to resist. When the German occupation forces rolled across into Hungary on 19 March they were followed by an advance party of the *Sonder Einsatzkommando* (Special

Operations Unit), and Eichmann with 140 trucks and command cars. On 21 March Eichmann was assigned temporary living quarters in the Hotel Majestic in the Schwabenberg district of Budapest. It would be from here that he would direct the fate of thousands of Hungarian Jews. Himmler now wanted the Hungarian Jews transported to Auschwitz where they would be selected for slave labour and shipped out again through various concentration camps that served German industry. Those selected for labour would be held in quarantine until transport was available to them. In effect, Himmler was planning to turn Auschwitz into a huge labour exchange just as he had done with the main camp in 1940, but now it was on a greater scale than ever before. The Auschwitz authorities were informed that they were to prepare for a huge assignment of Hungarian Jews. They were also told that more of an effort was to be made to separate those Jews who could serve the German war effort through work, but were to continue to use 'special treatment' on those that served absolutely no purpose for the Reich. Eichmann, who was in charge of transporting the Hungarian Jews directly to Auschwitz, began negotiating with the Hungarian police and helped organize the so-called ghettoization of the Jewish population in Hungary.

On 4 April Eichmann attended a conference to discuss ghettoization of the Hungarian Jews with the Hungarian authorities in Budapest. Between them they agreed to divide Hungary into six zones, and in these zones the Jews would be moved from the countryside into towns and cities. They would be stripped of their wealth and possessions and then moved to ghettos. The ghettos would be located close to rail lines for later transportation to the Reich 'for labour'. The operation would be undertaken by commanders of the Hungarian gendarmerie and the local police officials. It was agreed between Eichmann and the Hungarians that ghettoization should begin immediately and the deportations commence in the eastern provinces of the country first in order to reduce panic in Budapest. By leaving the Jews of the capital until last, the SS would lower the chances of possible Jewish resistance. After all, they did not want a repeat of the Warsaw uprising of April 1943.

In mid-April ghettoization commenced on the first day of the Jewish festival of Passover. With the people wearing the Yellow Star, which was made compulsory by law with the help of the new Hungarian government and authorities, ghettoization began in Zone I comprising Carpathian Ruthenia and north-eastern Hungary. Over a period of almost two weeks some 194,000 Jews were deported from their homes into 'ghettos' and holding camps. In early May, in Zone II including Kolozsvár/Cluj and northern Transylvania, 98,000 Jews were rounded up. Zone III comprising 53,000 Jews in northern Hungary were not moved until June along with Zone IV, which included Debrecen and Szeged in southern Hungary. Zone V in south-west Hungary where approximately 40,000 Jews were located would not be moved until late June and early July. During this period some 24,000 Jews in towns and villages on the outskirts of Budapest would be deported.

While ghettoization of the Hungarian Jews got under way in the last two weeks of April, the SS and Hungarian delegates continued to debate the fate of the Jews. Although Regent Nikolaus Horthy and Prime Minister Döme Sztójay consented to the shipment of 100,000 able-bodied Jews for labour in the Reich, the SS wanted to rid all the Jews from Hungarian soil, especially those unfit for labour. Following further talks about the deportation of Jews, a final decision was agreed on 22 April. Eichmann discussed timetables and ordering of railway carriages. It was approved that the first trains would start moving on 15 May and plans were arranged that a delivery of 3,000 Jews would be sent to Auschwitz each day. In order not to disrupt the war effort, 50,000 Jews in Budapest would not be deported in the first wave.

As preparations were made for the shipment of Hungarian Jews to Auschwitz, the SS personnel at Birkenau were already making plans to deal with the large transports. Rudolf Höss, who had been commandant of the camp up to late 1943, received a new commission from his superior *SS-Obergruppenführer* Oswald Pohl to return to the camp. Pohl ordered Höss not only to make preparations at the camp, but more importantly to find out how many Jews could still be expected for the armaments industry. Already Pohl had expanded the Auschwitz Empire into a system of satellite camps located on industrial sites. There was the Buna camp at Monowitz, the Jawischowitz camp near the mines at Brzeszcze, a small shoe factory camp in Chelmek and a number of other camps erected. In total there were 33,000 prisoners working in the satellite camps. The SS enterprises were very lucrative, taking an average of 2 million marks each month. Due to the sheer size of the enterprise, the command of Auschwitz-Birkenau and its satellite camps had been divided up into three command groups. Unfortunately, at the time of its transformation, Höss was not part of the master plan and was removed from his post as commandant.

On 1 December 1943 Höss joined the staff of Pohl's Economic Office and was appointed chief of Department DI: Central Office of the political section. He succeeded *SS-Standartenführer* Arthur Liebehenschel who had succeeded Höss as commandant of Auschwitz. In his new position Höss's main role was deputy of the inspector of the concentration camps. He enjoyed much broader powers and authority than he had at Auschwitz and believed he could improve the concentration camp system such as the overcrowding, deplorable sanitary conditions, the lack of building materials and to liaise with the commandants who had various issues.

In March 1944 Höss began receiving reports about deportation plans of Hungarian Jews to Auschwitz. Much of the information relating to the new deportation policy was regarding utilizing the Jews for slave labour. A month later in April Höss visited Heinrich Müller, chief of the RSHA (*Reichssicherheitshauptamt*: Reich Main Security Office). During their meeting they spoke at length about the pending operations in Hungary, but Müller was unable to give Höss any accurate figures, telling him he would have to journey to Budapest personally to meet with Eichmann. A couple of days later Höss left Berlin by train and travelled to the Hungarian capital where he met Eichmann in his Schwabenberg office. Sitting in his hotel office, Höss listened intently to Eichmann as he revealed the plans to uproot and deport almost 1 million people from Hungary. He told Höss that the Hungarian authorities had agreed on the deportation of the Jews and that the Hungarians could provide a large pool of slave labour at a time when the Reich was suffering acute shortages of manpower. Eichmann said he was responsible for rounding up the Hungarian Jews and deporting them to the Reich, and it was essential, as it had always been, that those fit were crucial for work and those unfit were to be exterminated. What made his job easier, he said, was the willingness of the Hungarians to cast out their Jewish compatriots so easily. However, despite the readiness of the Hungarian government to remove the Jews from its country, the operation was by no means an easy feat to achieve. He told Höss that it would take some considerable time to organize, so it was very important to reassure the Jews that nothing bad was going to happen to them. He confirmed that deportation plans had been made and the trains carrying more than 3,000 Jews each day would start arriving in Auschwitz sometime in May. The task, he said, was on an immense scale and because of the huge amount of rolling stock required, every effort had been made to ensure it would avoid disrupting the war effort. For this reason no Jews from Budapest would be transported to Auschwitz in the first wave. He hoped to deliver more than 760,000 Jews, almost 5 per cent of the population, to Auschwitz during the summer, but expected slightly less than the exaggerated figure. That evening Höss dined with Eichmann and the following day he departed Budapest bound for Berlin with all the necessary information for his boss, Pohl.

During late April and early May Höss made two more visits to Budapest where he consulted with Eichmann in preparation for the shipments to Auschwitz. During their private meetings Höss found Eichmann completely obsessed with his mission and was convinced more than ever that the Nazi war economy would benefit from the vast labour shipments to Auschwitz from Hungary. Those that could not work would be selected as normal and exterminated.

Upon Höss's return to Berlin he spoke at length with Pohl and highlighted the need of preparing Auschwitz for the transports. There had already been complaints about the running of the camp by the new commandants and Höss was keen to visit. On 7 May an order was sent from Himmler appointing Höss as commander of the overall SS garrison at Auschwitz. Himmler knew that Höss had transformed Auschwitz from a backwater concentration camp in the early 1940s to the largest killing facility in Europe. If anyone knew Auschwitz it was Höss, and for that reason he was given the job. Ever since his departure in November 1943, Höss had always shown a keen interest in returning to his old camp. While in his office in Berlin he had refused to sever all ties with the camp. Now he would be returning for a major operation never previously seen on any scale at Auschwitz and he relished the task ahead.

Reinhard Heydrich and Heinrich Müller (front row to the left) can be seen here with other Nazi officials in 1941. Heydrich was a high-ranking SS and police official and a main architect of the Holocaust. He was chief of the Reich Main Security Office and became deputy and acting Reich Protector of Bohemia and Moravia. He chaired the famous Wannsee Conference held in Berlin in January 1942, the purpose of which was to legalize the discrimination and removal of the Jewish race from existence in the occupied territories. Heydrich invited representatives from several government ministries, including state secretaries from the Foreign Office, the Justice, Interior and State Ministries and representatives from the SS.

A famous portrait photograph of *SS-Obersturmbannführer* Adolf Eichmann taken in 1942. Eichmann was one of the major organizers of the Holocaust: the 'Final Solution' to the Jewish question. He was tasked with facilitating and managing the logistics involved in the mass deportation of Jews to ghettos and extermination camps in Nazi-occupied Eastern Europe. Two years later in 1944 it was Eichmann who was charged with directing the fate of thousands of Hungarian Jews by train to Auschwitz.

Rudolf Höss can be seen here accompanying Heinrich Himmler on a tour of Auschwitz in the summer of 1942. It would be almost two years later in March 1944 that Himmler gave Höss full authority via orders from *SS-Obergruppenführer* Oswald Pohl for the destruction of the Hungarian Jews and to prepare their transportation to Auschwitz.

SS officers Oswald Pohl and Ernst-Heinrich Schmauser. Josef Kramer is pictured on the far left, partially obscured. The original caption reads: 'SS Ogrupf Pohl and Schmauser in Auschwitz 1944.' Pohl ordered Höss not only to make preparations at Auschwitz for the arrival of the Hungarian Jews, but to ensure that those fit for labour could be used in the armaments industry. This meant that mass selections would be carried out on the ramps first.

A portrait photograph of Heinrich Müller, chief of the RSHA (*Reichssicherheitshauptamt* or Reich Main Security Office). Müller also participated heavily in the planning of the removal of the Hungarian Jews from their homeland to Auschwitz.

SS-Reichsführer Himmler with Rudolf Höss. For the Hungarian mass transports Höss prepared the entire plan. He ordered that the expansion of the platform and the three-track rail connection into Birkenau be built as quickly as possible; also that pits be dug next to the crematorium and put back into operation including the previously inactive Bunker 2 and its pits. In the courtyard of the crematorium new signs were put up saying that new arrivals must bathe and be disinfected first.

Commandant *SS-Hauptsturmführer* Richard Baer (right) accompanies Oswald Pohl (left) during an official visit to Auschwitz by automobile. Baer and Höss under the supervision of Pohl worked very closely in planning the arrival of the Hungarian transports into the camp. (*USHMM*)

An aerial view showing Auschwitz-Birkenau in 1944. (*Auschwitz-Birkenau Museum/USHMM*)

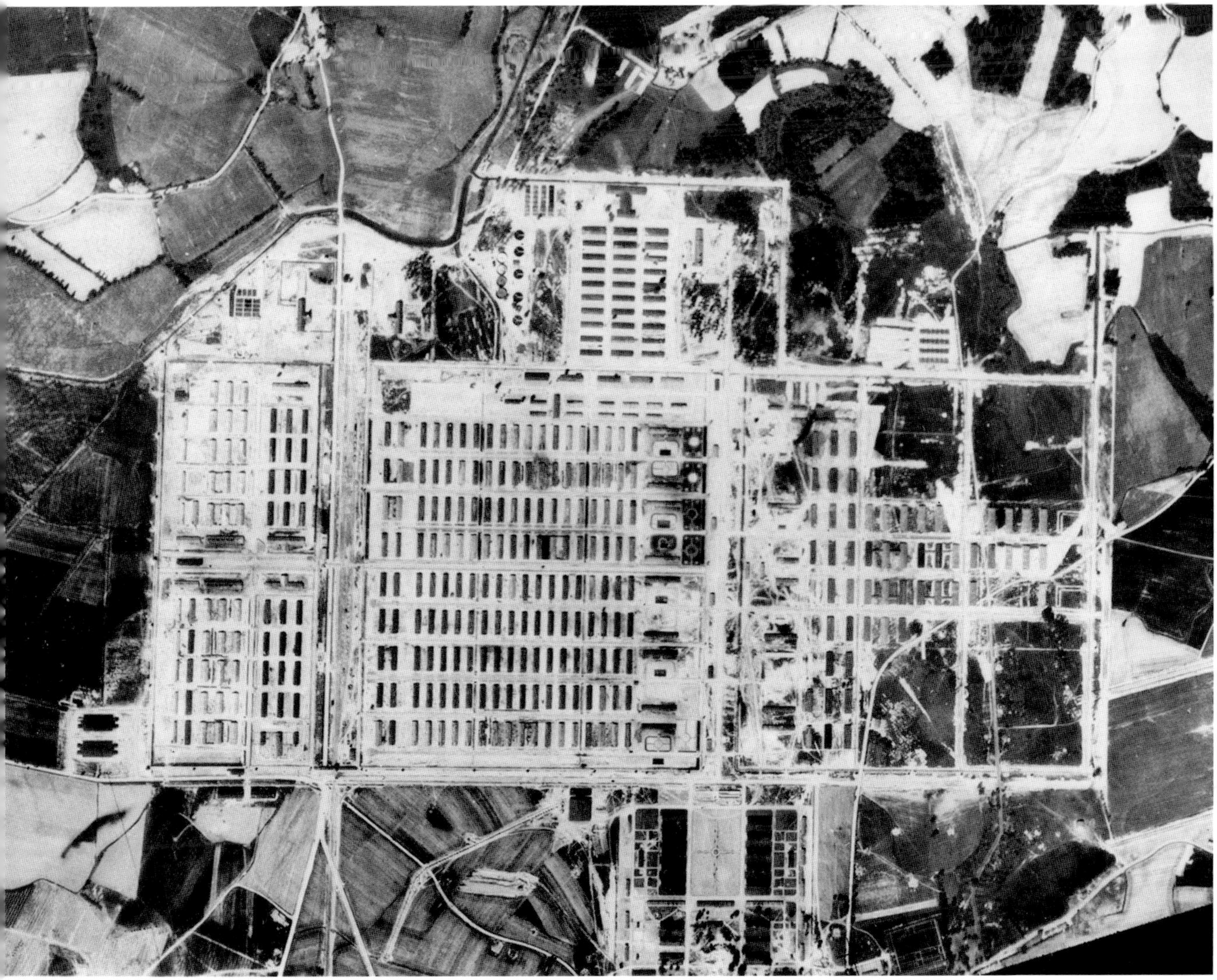

Chapter Two

Deportation

As preparations were put in place for the deportation of the Hungarian Jews, Eichmann and the Hungarian delegation toured the holding pens where the first shipments of Jews were waiting. They visited Kassa/Kosice, where about 12,000 Jews were crammed into two brick yards with hardly any shelter and a lack of sanitary facilities. In Ungvár/Uzhhorod 25,000 Jews were packed into a lumberyard and totally exposed to the elements, all of whom were totally stripped of their possessions. Hungry and with nothing to drink, they sat and endured days waiting for the cattle cars to take them into southern Poland to Auschwitz.

While the Jews waited to be transported, at Auschwitz on 8 May the new SS garrison commander Rudolf Höss arrived in the main camp. It did not take long before he got himself formally acquainted with the camp once again. The day he arrived, the commandant of Auschwitz I, *SS-Obersturmbannführer* Arthur Liebehenschel was relieved of his command. He was replaced by *SS-Hauptsturmführer* Richard Baer. Höss and Baer worked very closely together. A lot had changed at Auschwitz-Birkenau since Höss's departure. Liebehenschel had divided the camp into three independent sectors, giving *SS-Sturmbannführer* Friedrich Wilhelm Heinrich Hartjenstein the largest part to command which was Birkenau. Both men had worked well together, but like Liebehenschel, Hartjenstein was not a brutal commander. During Höss's inspection of Birkenau with Baer, he was perturbed by the general running of the camp and filed a dissatisfied report to Berlin. When Eichmann arrived from Budapest to make a formal inspection of Birkenau for the transports to commence, he was incensed that Hartjenstein had not fulfilled his orders. Though the incineration installations at Crematorium V were not properly in service because the ovens were being filled with special fireclay paste, the open-air cremation ditches that had been hastily dug behind the gas chamber in order to compensate for the low incineration output were standing idle. As a result, the gassed victims were piled up outside waiting to be burned. It was decided that Hartjenstein would be relieved of his command and transferred as commandant to the Natzweiler concentration camp in the Alsace region of France. Hartenstein's replacement was none other than Höss's first ever adjutant and an old veteran of the concentration camp system,

SS-Hauptsturmführer Josef Kramer. Kramer arrived at Auschwitz on 8 May where he immediately took up his duties as the new *Lagerführer* of Auschwitz II-Birkenau.

Living conditions in the Birkenau camp were as bad as ever, with disease and plagues of rats everywhere. The stench of faeces, urine and filth coupled with the constant smell of burning corpses made every newcomer sick to their stomach. With the immense overcrowding and the severe lack of food, hundreds were perishing every day. Yet in spite of the terrible conditions, Höss had no time to think about the welfare of the living as he was already busy making preparations for the arrival of the Hungarian Jews.

On 15 May, almost one month after the ghettoization of the Hungarian Jews commenced, the Jews of Zones I and II were herded 'like animals' by the Hungarian gendarmerie from their ghettos of Kassa, Ungvár, Munkacs and other holding areas towards the rail lines where trains were waiting. Under the supervision of Hungarian police officials, Jewish men, women and children arrived at the rail heads and were packed into the cattle cars. For three days, with the cars sealed, the Jews had to endure the journey without food, water or sanitation. As a result of the horrendous conditions, hundreds of old people and the sick, including the very young, died before they even reached Birkenau.

In preparation for the first Hungarian shipment at the camp Höss had already set to work and ordered that Crematorium V be put into operation again. An engineer's report, however, confirmed that the Crematorium V furnaces were still damaged, and because of their slow incineration rate they had replaced them in late April with five small incineration ditches. In order to compensate for the huge numbers of transports expected over the coming weeks, it was suggested to reactivate Bunker II, which was taken out of operation around April/May 1943, and designate it as Bunker 2/V. Bunker II had been a cottage known as the 'Little White House' and converted in June 1942 to what the SS called a 'bathing facility for special actions'. The interior of the cottage comprised four narrow rooms that were constructed as gas chambers. With better ventilation and a killing capacity of around 1,200 people at any one time, Höss was sure that Bunker II would accelerate the number of people they needed to kill. However, because of his past experiences at the camp, it was not actually the process of killing the Jews that presented him and his SS colleagues with any problems; the hardest task was disposing of the gassed victims. So that he could facilitate the process of murdering the Hungarian Jews more quickly and effectively, he put *SS-Hauptsturmführer* Otto Moll in charge of all four crematoria and assigned a special squad to enlarge the insides of them. From Crematoria V a special track was laid between the building and the pits so that the corpses could be loaded onto trolleys and disposed of quickly. As for the other killing installations, they were also overhauled including Crematoria II and III, which received new elevators connecting the gas chambers with the incineration rooms. Even the walls of the changing rooms and the gas chambers were given a fresh coat of paint.

To assist with the smooth arrival of the Hungarian Jews and to provide a direct link between Auschwitz station and the crematoria the train lines were extended through the main entrance of Birkenau with plans to run them right up to Crematoria II and III. Night and day hundreds of prisoners had been busy laying the three-way railway track through the camp and constructing the loading and unloading ramps. By the second week of May the railway line was completed and the finishing touches were made to the ramps. From these ramps Höss would then coordinate the destruction of the Hungarian Jews, now code-named Operation HÖSS or *Aktion Höss*.

Jews have been removed from their ghetto and escorted by Hungarian gendarmerie for transportation by rail car to Auschwitz-Birkenau. The commencement of the shipment of Hungarian Jews was undertaken with the help of the Hungarian authorities, particularly the gendarmerie. The plan was to use 45 cattle cars per train on 4 trains a day to deport 12,000 Jews from the countryside every day, starting in mid-May 1944.

Hungarian men are shown on a loading ramp preparing to be sent directly to Auschwitz-Birkenau under the supervision of Hungarian gendarmerie and soldiers. During early May 1944 under the supervision of Hungarian police officials, orders were sent out that all Jewish men, women and children were to be removed from their ghettos or temporary holding areas, sent to the railheads and packed into the cattle cars.

Jewish men, women and children are seen here preparing to be loaded on a waiting train. The planning of the shipments of Hungarian Jews to Auschwitz was a huge undertaking and included extensive help from the Hungarian railroad authorities.

Here 1,800 Jews are being loaded onto cattle cars and transported from the Kristaca Camp in May 1944.

German soldiers are supervising the Jewish transport from a loading ramp in the summer of 1944. Men and children have all their possessions with them, which would be immediately confiscated upon their arrival at Auschwitz.

(**Opposite**) Jews from Dunaszerdahely are seen here on a very warm day on 15 June 1944 being loaded onto a cattle car. A wooden ramp is assisting an elderly gentleman. On 10 May an order had been sent out to the Hungarian authorities to construct a Jewish ghetto in Dunaszerdahely. Almost a month later on 8 June, the Jews from the ghetto were told to leave their dwellings with belongings where they were escorted and herded into the Great Synagogue and adjacent buildings. Between 13 and 15 June the Jews were then led to the main rail hub where they were deported to Auschwitz on two transports. This photograph was taken during the second deportation. (*Yad Vashem*)

(**Above**) Jewish men, women and children are seen here being loaded onto a cattle car. The deportations were so immense that the planning was coordinated by various German government ministries and state organizations, including the Reich Security Main Office (RSHA), the Transport Ministry and Foreign Office including Hungarian government officials. The RSHA coordinated and directed the deportations; the Transport Ministry organized train schedules with the Hungarian train authorities; the Foreign Office negotiated with the Hungarian government about handing over their Jews. (*Auschwitz-Birkenau*)

(**Opposite, above**) The deportation of Jews from the Körmend ghetto is seen here at a station for their debarkation on 19 June 1944. The Körmend ghetto was erected only a month earlier to temporarily hold the Hungarian Jews before they were marched out and transported to the much larger Szombathely ghetto. Carrying suitcases and bundles of possessions, they were escorted by gendarmes on foot through the town to the railway station, where they were transported to Szombathely. It would be on 3 July that the vast majority of Jews from Szombathely were deported to Auschwitz. Some 3,000 people were crammed into forty-seven cattle cars.

(**Opposite, below**) Here Jews from Kőszeg are led through the town bound for the railhead to be transported to Auschwitz.

(**Above**) In Kőszeg a group of Jews are seen on the loading ramp being prepared for deportation to Auschwitz under the supervision of the Hungarian gendarmerie. Jews of Kőszeg were among the last to be deported to the death camp in the summer of 1944.

Chapter Three

Arrival

More than 6,300 Hungarian Jews had boarded the first two transports from the ghettos of Nyíregyháza and Munkacs. This first major transport steamed its way through to Auschwitz on 15 May 1944, arriving the next day ahead of schedule because the journey had been unhindered by local partisans or enemy aircraft. The deportation schedule outlined for three or four trains each day. The victims were crammed in seventy to ninety per freight car with two buckets, one filled with water and the other empty for excrement. Each train was accompanied and guarded by Hungarian gendarmes until their arrival in Kassa, where they were replaced by SS personnel.

Once the transport arrived the train pulled over the new spur through the gate into Birkenau and halted at the ramps. Waiting at the ramps were SS personnel and *Sonderkommando*, which assisted in the unloading of the victims. When the box car doors of the train were opened many personnel frequently complained of the stale smell of sweat, urine and excrement. The state of some of the cars was appalling, with a number of people, especially the old and very young, already dying. Those that had survived often arrived hungry and with a raging thirst. Their condition was carefully planned by the SS and was aimed at subduing the new arrivals. Consequently many of the victims were so preoccupied with the thought of water that they often could not focus on their surroundings. At the ramps they stood in a weakened state, especially the old. The weather was particularly hot and this increased their craving for water. An SS officer often could be heard calling out across the mass exodus of people spilling across onto the ramps waiting to be selected and 'processed', promising them water and soup after the 'disinfecting showers'.

The camp personnel had all been given explicit instructions that the process from unloading to murder had to be undertaken at rapid speed if they were to achieve the desired result. At Auschwitz they had mastered calm and speed as a means of ensuring a smooth functioning for the processing of their new arrivals. On the ramp there was a hive of activity as the newcomers were crammed together. Most of them did not suspect anything. Nothing seemed to indicate the horror that was in store for them. Many believed that they had simply arrived at a new camp to be contained and worked before they were perhaps moved on further east. Before they were disinfected they were kindly requested to leave their luggage on the ramp and hand in all their money and valuables. For Höss and his subordinates processing in an atmosphere of great calm was the easiest and most practical means of duping the Jews. Each member of the camp was trained to trick all new arrivals into believing they had alighted at a temporary holding-point where they would work and have food, and that they would be treated as a precaution against disease.

Once the Jews were unloaded onto the ramps they were immediately separated into two columns: one of women and children; the other of men. A selection was then carried out by one or two SS medical doctors and the two columns were divided into four: two of women and children and two of men. Those unfit for labour were sent straight ahead towards the crematoria, while all able-bodied workers were interned in Auschwitz or were retained ready at a moment's notice to be transferred to other camps in the Reich. The selection for labour in each transport varied daily: sometimes it was as low as 10 per cent or as high as 50 per cent, but the majority of Jews that arrived through the gates of Birkenau were immediately sent through to their deaths. There were roughly 3,300 people per day arriving, and sometimes that figure even rose to 4,300. On 20 May, for instance, one convoy arrived with an average of 3,000 people of whom some 1,000 were able and 2,000 unable to work. The following day on 21 May two convoys were reported to have arrived from Hungary with 6,000 people of whom 2,000 were able to work and the remainder were directly sent to their deaths. Shipments to the camp varied daily, and some days trains actually queued to get into the camp and unload their human cargo.

Records of the train arrivals were catalogued and from the very beginning of Operation HÖSS until midnight on 28 May, it was reported that some 184,049 Jews had arrived in Auschwitz in 58 trains. A couple of weeks later on 13 June a report was filed that a total of 289,357 Jews had been 'transported to their destination' from the allocated Hungarian Zones I and II in 92 trains, each with 45 freight cars. The transportation of Hungarian Jews in Zone III was not completed until 30 June, comprising some 50,805 Jews. The arrivals list stated that as of 1 July a total of 340,162 Hungarian Jews had arrived. With the completion of the Hungarian Zone IV, the number of deportees totalled 381,661. Finally, with the liquidation of Jews from Zone V, mainly from western Hungary and the southern suburbs of Budapest, it was reported on 9 July that 55,471 Jews had arrived. This figure increased the final number of Jews that had arrived to 437,402.

During the midst of these Hungarian transports there were calls to Eichmann for labour shipments to Austria because there was a general pressure from many bodies to stop or at least slow down the rapid rate of killing. Another concern was the reaction in the West regarding reports of Raoul Wallenberg, the Swedish envoy in Budapest. In order to quell further protests from Wallenberg, Eichmann offered a deal to the successful Hungarian-Jewish lawyer and journalist Rudolf Kasztner to put

30,000 Jews 'on ice'. Kasztner, who was also the founding member of the Budapest Aid and Rescue Committee, agreed but had to pay the SS a huge fee in cash. The deal was made and transports of Jews probably left Hungary for Strasshof in Austria after 16 June and possibly also after 25 June.

Another deal was done between Kasztner and Eichmann to allow 1,600 Hungarian Jews to escape Auschwitz in exchange for gold, diamonds and cash. Around 150 of the wealthiest Jews paid $1,500 each to cover their own and the others' escape. The trains, known by the SS as 'Kasztner trains', spent a gruelling seven weeks travelling including a temporary diversion to the Bergen-Belsen concentration camp. Surviving passengers would reach Switzerland in August and December 1944.

Those Jews that were unfortunate enough not to be diverted across Europe would steam their way directly to Auschwitz-Birkenau. Logistically the transports were a huge undertaking, not just the shipments by train from Hungary to southern Poland but the mammoth task of dealing with the new arrivals inside Birkenau. For the camp personnel receiving the many thousands of people each day, efficiency was key to its successful running.

Once all arrivals had been unloaded, they were quickly processed. What was left in the wake of every transport was masses of personal belongings littering the ramps. One primary group of people tasked with collecting valuables and clothing were the 'clearing-up commandos' or *Aufraumungskommando*. These special units confiscated property of the transports and sorted them for storage in the warehouse complex known as 'Kanada'. Höss himself, including some of his camp personnel and management, also adopted this term. The members of this 'clearing-up commando' were almost exclusively Jews. 'Kanada' storage facilities occupied several dozen barracks and other buildings around the camp, and some 1,500 prisoners worked there in two shifts sorting through all the plundered Jewish goods. The barracks were literally a treasure trove to the individual members of the SS. They had seen nothing like it, and many of them were unable to resist the temptation provided by these 'riches'. Supervision of the SS in 'Kanada' was surprisingly slack and as a result many actively participated in theft. SS officers at Auschwitz were also personally benefiting from the accumulating wealth. Diamonds, gold, coins and Hungarian currency was stolen. Large amounts of food and alcohol were also taken for personal use and sold on the black market. The bulk of the property was stored in the 'Kanada' stores, sorted and then funnelled from Auschwitz through an extensive distribution network that served many individuals and various economic branches of the Nazi regime.

(**Above**) Here Hungarian Jews have arrived at Birkenau and disembark from the cattle cars to await selection. While the fear of arriving at the camp was widespread, their journey by train was long, arduous and the conditions appalling. Even in 1944, the Nazis disguised their 'Final Solution' as the 'mass resettlement to the east'. *(Yad Vashem)*

(**Opposite, above**) Old men and women can be seen here disembarking from the cattle cars at Birkenau. Mothers are seen with their children walking along the ramp for selection. This ramp, known as the 'third ramp', was built inside Birkenau and went into operation in May 1944. It was built purely in connection with the anticipated arrival of transports of Hungarian Jews. *(Yad Vashem)*

(**Opposite, below**) As Jews unload from a cattle car, a crowd of men, women and children wait before they are called and selected.

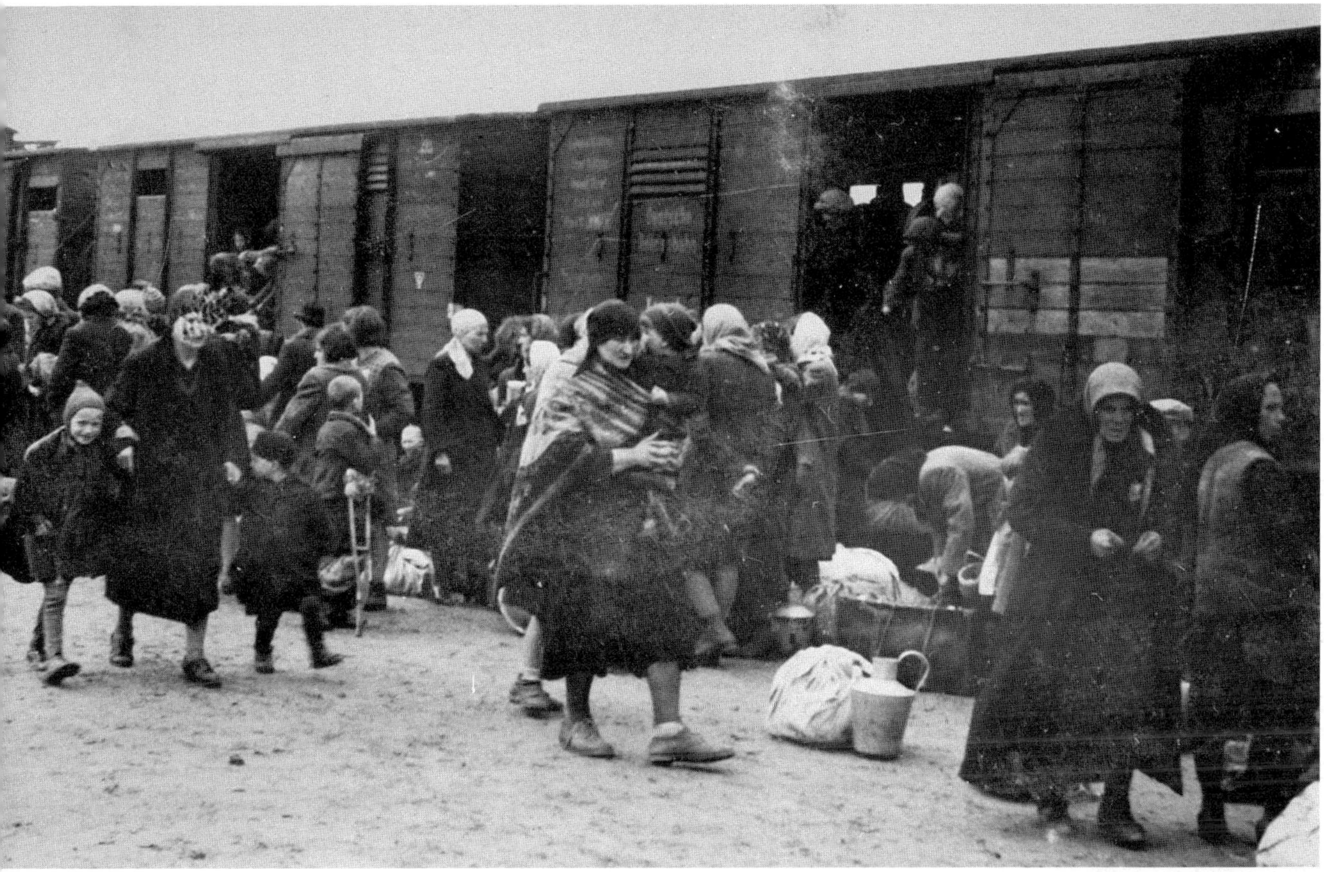

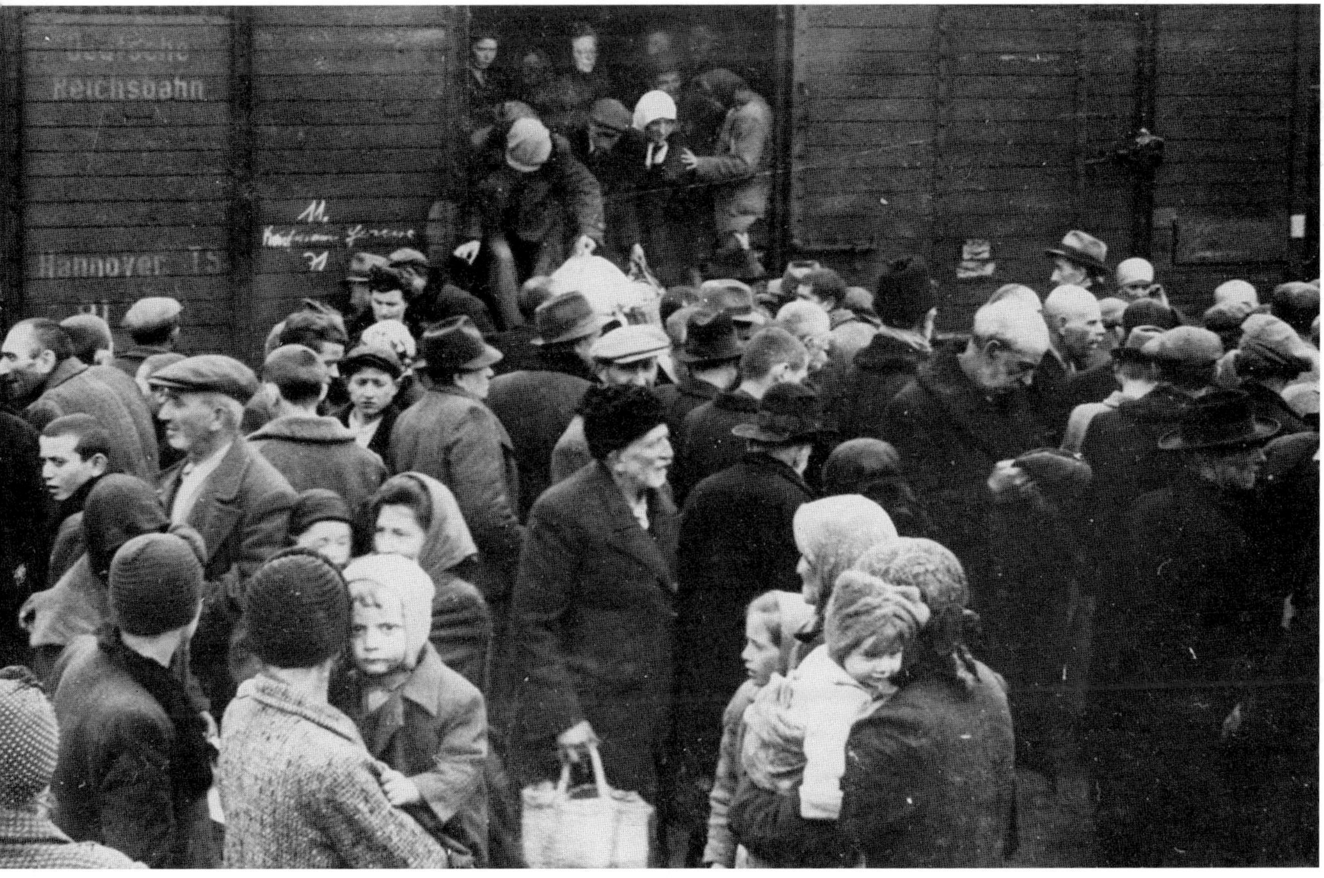
Reichsbahn
Hannover 15

(**Opposite**) Two photographs taken in sequence of the mass debarkation of Jewish men, women and children, all holding onto their bundles of belongings. The journey to the camp could often last for days in appalling insanitary conditions. Although there was widespread relief on arriving, the stress and fear of what would happen to them can only be imagined. Note in the distance (left to right) are Crematoria II and III. (*Yad Vashem/Auschwitz-Birkenau Museum*)

(**Above**) Hundreds of Jewish men, women and children can be seen on the ramp waiting for selection. Two ladies, one smiling, wave to get the attention of someone they obviously recognize. It's quite evident that many did not know their fate. Note German officers and guards congregating to prepare for the selection process. The prisoners, dressed in the familiar striped concentration camp garments, were tasked with collecting valuables and clothing. These were known as 'clearing-up commandos' or *Aufraumungskommando*. They were also known as 'Kanada Kommando'. These special units confiscated the property of the transports and sorted it for storage in the warehouse complex known as 'Kanada'. In the distance is Crematoria II. (*Yad Vashem/Auschwitz-Birkenau Museum*)

A throng of men, women and children are seen after disembarking from their transport. They would have been told to leave their possessions on the ramp so they could be selected and taken to the showers to be cleaned. The trucks on the service road which leads down to the gates at Crematoria II and III were mainly used for collecting the personal possessions left on the ramp. They sometimes assisted in transporting those people too old or sick to walk to the gas chambers. *(Yad Vashem/Auschwitz-Birkenau Museum)*

Jews disembarking from a cattle car, still clutching their possessions. Some of the people can clearly be seen wearing the Star of David stitched to the left breast of their clothing. *(Yad Vashem/Auschwitz-Birkenau Museum)*

Jewish men and women are seen here with their belongings, flanked by members of the 'clearing-up commandos'. *(Yad Vashem/Auschwitz-Birkenau Museum)*

(**Opposite, above**) A number of old men and women rest next to a cattle car following their long and strenuous journey to the camp. *(Yad Vashem/Auschwitz-Birkenau Museum)*

(**Opposite, below**) Here we see hundreds of men, women and children waiting on the ramp in preparation for their selection. In the distance is Crematorium II. *(Yad Vashem/Auschwitz-Birkenau Museum)*

(**Above**) Once the Jewish people had disembarked from the train and discarded their bundles of possessions in bags and suitcases, the selection process was undertaken on the ramp. Hundreds of men, women and children were separated. All families were divided after leaving the train and all the people were lined up in two columns. The men and older boys were in one column, and the women and children of both sexes in the other. In this photograph a German officer is pointing and preparing the columns. After the selection process the people were led to the camp doctors and other camp functionaries. They judged the people standing before them on sight, and sometimes those being selected had to give a brief statement as to their age and occupation. This decided whether they would live or die. Note in the distance the long column of people trudging along the service road towards Crematoria II and III. They have all been selected to be processed for death. *(Yad Vashem/Auschwitz-Birkenau Museum)*

(**Opposite, above**) A column of men appeared to have been selected for labour. The process of being chosen to live would mean the people would be escorted to the General Sauna, showered, cleaned and their hair shaved.
(*Yad Vashem/Auschwitz-Birkenau Museum*)

(**Opposite, below**) This photograph shows the selection of a male column. Whole families often arrived in Auschwitz, but soon after their arrival they were parted from one another and forced to make two separate lines.
(*Yad Vashem/Auschwitz-Birkenau Museum*)

(**Above & overleaf**) Five photographs showing Jewish men from Subcarpathian Rus awaiting selection on the ramp. In May 1944, Hungarian authorities deported some 140,000 Jews from the southern areas of Slovakia and Subcarpathian Rus to the border of the Government General in Poland held by German authorities. The SS and police officials then deported them directly to Auschwitz-Birkenau, the majority of them being selected for death.
(*Yad Vashem/Auschwitz-Birkenau Museum*)

(**Opposite**) Two photographs showing a large group of Subcarpathian Rus Jews queuing, waiting for selection. Höss outlined to his SS staff that the trains coming to the ramp in Birkenau consisted of forty to fifty freight cars: 'After the selection the boys and healthy individuals, without being recorded in the camp registers, are admitted to the camp as so-called depot prisoners. The remaining people are sent to the gas chambers.' *(Yad Vashem/Auschwitz-Birkenau Museum)*

(**Above**) Jewish men and boys are seen here queuing along the ramp during a selection process. For the SS at Birkenau age was a very important criterion during this process. Due to the high demand for labour, healthy children as young as 14 years old were selected in the summer of 1944. *(Yad Vashem/Auschwitz-Birkenau Museum)*

(**Above**) Jewish brothers from Subcarpathian Rus are awaiting selection on the ramp. Pictured here are Israel and Zelig Jacob, aged 9 and 11. Sadly, they were selected for death shortly after this photograph was taken. (*Yad Vashem/Auschwitz-Birkenau Museum*)

(**Opposite & overleaf**) Four photographs showing Jewish women and children from Subcarpathian Rus awaiting selection. It is certain that the majority of these people were selected for death. All mothers, pregnant women, the elderly and those in poor health would be gassed. As a statistical average, only about 20 per cent of the people in these transports were chosen for labour. (*Yad Vashem/Auschwitz-Birkenau Museum*)

Six photographs showing Jewish men from Subcarpathian Rus awaiting selection on the ramp. Many of the men in the photograph appear elderly. SS medical personnel would sadly send them to the gas chambers where they were usually killed and cremated on the same day. *(Yad Vashem/Auschwitz-Birkenau Museum)*

An elderly Jewish man from Subcarpathian Rus sits at the side of the ramp awaiting his fate before he is called for selection.
(Yad Vashem/Auschwitz-Birkenau Museum)

Men are shown here awaiting selection. During May 1944 some 3,300 Jews were arriving in the camp every day, but this figure rose as high as 4,300 on occasion. On 20 May, for instance, a convoy was carrying approximately 3,000 people, of whom only 1,000 were fit for labour. The following day two convoys arrived carrying 6,000 people, of whom only 2,000 were selected as fit for labour.
(Yad Vashem/Auschwitz-Birkenau Museum)

Four photographs showing Jewish women from Subcarpathian Rus awaiting selection. Many of these females look like they would have been selected for labour as they appear young, healthy and do not have children with them.
(Yad Vashem/Auschwitz-Birkenau Museum)

Two photographs showing the selection process on the ramp. Selection was made by SS officers like Dr Fritz Klein, a fanatical Nazi, who testified in Allied captivity in 1945 about his time as a Birkenau camp physician. He said: 'When transports arrived at Auschwitz it was the doctor's job to pick out those who were unfit or unable to work. These included children, old people and the sick. I have seen the gas chambers and crematoria at Auschwitz, and I knew that those I selected were to go to the gas chamber. But I only acted on orders given by chief SS physician Dr Wirth...' The selection was carried out exclusively by doctors. One looked at the person and, if she looked ill, asked a few questions, but if the person was healthy then it was decided immediately. *(Yad Vashem/Auschwitz-Birkenau Museum)*

(**Above**) Two female Jews from Subcarpathian Rus have been selected for labour and walk off to be bathed and disinfected. *(Yad Vashem/Auschwitz-Birkenau Museum)*

(**Opposite, above**) SS guards walk along the arrival ramp following a transportation of Hungarian Jews. What follows is the clearing-up operation by the 'Kanada Kommandos'. The Birkenau arrival ramp was completed only weeks before this photograph was taken. Prior to the third ramp being constructed the deportation trains arrived at a ramp that was half a mile away. Now trains could pull into Birkenau, allowing the killing machine to be operated more efficiently. Crematoria II and III can be seen in the far background. *(Yad Vashem/Auschwitz-Birkenau Museum)*

(**Opposite, below**) A view of a mound of confiscated personal property from an arriving transport of Jews from Subcarpathian Rus. *(Yad Vashem/Auschwitz-Birkenau Museum)*

(**Opposite, above**) 'Kanada Kommandos' can be seen here at the ramp clearing the possessions of the Jews. For the Hungarian operation Höss ordered that the number of clearing-up commandos be increased. This meant that prisoners who were working in the crematoria and in 'Kanada' warehouses be brought out into the camp to assist in the sorting of the Jewish property left at the ramp. (*Yad Vashem/Auschwitz-Birkenau Museum*)

(**Opposite, below**) The mass of possessions left on the ramp are being sorted by the 'Kanada Kommandos'. In preparing for the Hungarian arrivals Höss had deduced that the time required to unload a train with people and their entire baggage was four to five hours per transport. 'No transport had been processed in less than this time,' he said. The people could be processed within this time, but there would be such a vast quantity of baggage that there was no way both the German and Hungarian train authorities would be able to enlarge the transports, despite the sorting squads being reinforced with 1,000 additional prisoners. (*Yad Vashem/Auschwitz-Birkenau Museum*)

(**Above**) Prisoners in the *Aufraumungskommando* (order commandos) and nicknamed 'Kanada Kommandos' sort through a mound of personal belongings confiscated from the arriving transport of Jews from Subcarpathian Rus. The primary tasks of these special units were to assist in camp duties such as unloading Jews from trains with the assistance of the order commandos (*Aufraumungskommando*), a group of recruited Jews who were used to unload the confiscated property of the transports. They were tasked with collecting transport possessions and sorting them for storage in the warehouse complex known as 'Kanada'. (*Yad Vashem/Auschwitz-Birkenau Museum*)

(**Opposite, above**) A cart is being hauled here by 'Kanada Kommandos' containing numerous pots and pans. Note the volume of bags of possessions being unloaded from two transport vehicles at one of the 'Kanada' warehouses. (*USHMM/Yad Vashem*)

(**Opposite, below**) Prisoners in the 'Kanada Kommandos' unload the confiscated property of a transport of Jews. The camp prisoners came to refer to the looted property as 'Kanada', associating it with the riches symbolized by Canada. The members of this commando were almost exclusively Jews. 'Kanada' storage facilities occupied several dozen barracks and other buildings around the camp. The looted property was funnelled from Auschwitz through an extensive distribution network that served many individuals and various economic branches of the Third Reich. (*USHMM/Yad Vashem*)

(**Above**) Masses of possessions from the Hungarian arrivals are being unloaded here from a transport vehicle at one of the 'Kanada' warehouses. There were some thirty wooden buildings near the gas chambers in the BIIg section of Birkenau that stored all the possessions of the arrivals. Situated in this area were also two barracks for the 'Kanada Kommandos' and one for the SS who worked there. (*USHMM/Yad Vashem*)

(**Above**) 'Kanada Kommandos' unload the confiscated property of a transport of murdered Jews from Subcarpathian Rus at a warehouse. Note the vehicle is carrying clothing, most likely from recently murdered victims. (*USHMM/Yad Vashem*)

(**Opposite, above**) Clothing from a Hungarian transport being unloaded from a vehicle. On 22 July 1944, 210 male prisoners worked in Kanada I and 590 in Kanada II. (*USHMM/Yad Vashem*)

(**Opposite, below**) The first of three photographs showing 'Kanada Kommandos' sorting possessions from transport vehicles. Prisoners who worked in 'Kanada' were regarded as privileged. They were able to obtain extra rations and clothing from the possessions; items that could save their lives, especially in the harsh conditions of the camp. Some of these prisoners also performed other duties in the camp. In order to speed the arrival of the Hungarian shipments some were drafted into duties on the ramp where they opened up the doors of the cattle cars when the new transports arrived. Here they helped the deportees disembark, and then under the strict supervision of the SS they arranged the men and women into separate columns consisting of rows of five. They gathered the luggage scattered on the ramp and left in the cattle cars, loaded everything onto transport vehicles and moved the freight to the Kanada warehouses. The sorting began here: suitcases and bags were opened and the objects were thoroughly searched and sorted by type. (*USHMM/Yad Vashem*)

Two photographs showing female commandos sorting the huge piles of possessions for the 'Kanada' stores. By mid-July the majority of the warehouses were at full capacity and as a result thousands of items of clothing, shoes, wicker baskets and kitchen ware were often piled outside. *(USHMM/Yad Vashem)*

(**Opposite, above**) 'Kanada Kommandos' loading bags of possessions into the Barrack 5 warehouse. Although the shipment process took roughly five hours from arrival, selection and clearing the ramp and sorting the huge amounts of belongings was a massive undertaking. Often teams were unable to complete the assignments and overlapped with other arrivals' possessions. (USHMM/Yad Vashem)

(**Opposite, below**) Women inmates sort through a huge pile of shoes from the transport of Hungarian Jews. (USHMM/Yad Vashem)

(**Above**) 'Kanada Kommandos' sorting belongings from a shipment. From the end of May as more transports from Hungary arrived, Höss ordered hundreds of Hungarian Jewish women to be assigned to preliminary work details in Kanada II, where in the summer of 1944 an average of 1,500 to 2,000 women and men performed work duties. The warehouses of Kanada II in BIIg were located between Crematoria III and IV. Here prisoners working had a good vantage point to personally witness the gassing procedure in Crematorium V as well as in the reactivated temporary gas chamber (Bunker 2). (USHMM/Yad Vashem)

(**Above**) A view of one of the warehouses, overflowing with clothes confiscated from Hungarian transports into the camp. (*NARA*)

(**Opposite, above**) Female 'Kanada Kommandos' unload the confiscated property of a transport of Jews from Subcarpathian Rus at a warehouse. Many Hungarian women working in 'Kanada' called it 'the *Brezinka*' or *Brezsinka* because of the orchard of birches (in Polish *brzezinka*) surrounding the camp. (*USHMM/Yad Vashem*)

(**Opposite, below**) A column of transport vehicles carrying possessions destined to be sorted at the Kanada warehouses passes a line of Hungarian females that have been selected for labour. (*USHMM/Yad Vashem*)

Elderly Jews from Subcarpathian Rus who have been selected for death wait to be transported to the gas chambers. Surrounding them are masses of possessions piled up waiting to be loaded onto trucks to the nearby Kanada warehouses. (*USHMM/Yad Vashem*)

Chapter Four

Slave Labour

It was estimated that 10–20 per cent of the people arriving on the ramps at Auschwitz-Birkenau were selected for labour. Once selected, the process was undertaken very quickly as SS personnel were mindful to segregate those that were chosen to live from those that were selected to die. Often in double file, the hand-picked labourers were sorted into males and females and the individual sexes were led into the camp, registered as prisoners and assigned the next numbers in the various series. They were then escorted to the 'Central Sauna' brick building at the bottom of the camp. Its primary role was to carry out sanitary operations on all incoming able-bodied transports. Those that entered the building facility were undressed, had their hair cut, received a medical examination, were disinfected and then showered. They were then given prisoner uniforms made of coarse grey-blue striped material and clogs, which were standard issue in the concentration camp system, before being marched to their allocated wooden stable-type barracks.

From there they were given their tasks and put into gangs. These tasks ranged from loading heavy materials to producing chemicals, mining, weapons and fuel or building. Others were put into special sorting gangs or the 'clearing-up commandos'. Some men were rounded up and forced into the *Sonderkommandos* where they would have to work in the crematoria and assist in the incineration and corpse disposal.

Slave labour at Auschwitz had been very lucrative for the SS and they looked upon the new arrivals of Hungarians as increasing productivity. By May 1944 there were already thousands of prisoners working in the satellite camps. Many of the Hungarian Jews that were chosen for work detail often ended up working in the satellite camps. On 29 May, for instance, Hungarian inmates with A-series serial numbers were transferred to Monowitz, which was also known as Monowitz-Buna, Buna and Auschwitz III. In late 1942 the SS had established the camp at the request of IG Farben executives to provide slave labour for their Buna Werke industrial complex. The factory produced synthetic rubber for the war. In 1944 some 11,000 people were working at the factory complex as slave labour. Gangs of labourers were sorted into work *Kommandos*, which ranged from several hundred prisoners to a handful. Each *Kommando* had its own reference number and a name specifying the location or type of work.

Nearby other German industrial enterprises had built factories with their own sub-camps, such as Siemens-Schuckert's Bobrek complex and Krupp, all profiting from the use of slave labour. Again gangs were made up of work *Kommandos*. Their work details were often gruelling and under terrible conditions. The work was diverse and consisted of the transfer of construction materials, earthworks, transport of narrow-gauge railway wagons filled with earth and the laying of power cables. Some even worked as carpenters, roofers, painters and electricians.

After work the prisoners returned to the camp in the columns. Before 1944 there was a roll-call, but because there were so many people in the camp this practice was abandoned. The harsh work, poor nutrition and the general conditions in the sub-camps resulted in many of the slave labourers being sent to Birkenau to be gassed.

It was not just the Auschwitz satellite camps where newly-arrived Hungarian labourers were sent to work. On 5 June 2,000 were sent to the Buchenwald concentration camp in Germany. Many were worked in the female satellite camps in Mühlhausen, Gotha, Buttelstedt, Essen, Lippstadt, Weimar, Penig and numerous other sites. A week later on 13 June a shipment of some 2,000 was sent to Mauthausen and hundreds more were later transported. They were intended for tunnel construction at St Georgen and were mostly housed in camp Gusen II. The mortality rate among this group of prisoners was huge. Within months more than 2,100 of the 3,500 Hungarian Jewish prisoners at Gusen died there or were brought to Hartheim to be gassed.

Elsewhere across the Reich, the need for labour continued to be desperate. Although Eichmann was determined to transport as many Hungarian Jews to Auschwitz as possible, a considerable number were not deported to the camp but to Austria. In June 1944, more than 15,000 Jews were diverted from being sent to Birkenau to Vienna and Lower Austria for slave labour. Many more were later transported. Thousands of Hungarians comprising whole families, which would have met their fate at Auschwitz, were sent to Austria where they were urgently needed as manpower in factories and on farms. The deported families – mainly mothers, children and grandparents – had to work on farms, in construction companies, bread factories or oil refineries, all as forced labourers.

As for the majority of Hungarian Jews, they were transported directly to Auschwitz-Birkenau and those fit for labour were forced to work more than eleven hours with scarcely any rest or proper tools, often under brutal conditions. Even though the labour force was desperately required, the Nazis still pursued their policy of 'annihilation through work' under which certain categories of prisoners were sometimes worked to death. This policy meant that many of the camp prisoners were forced to work while lacking sufficient food, clothing, shelter or medical care that would directly and deliberately lead to illness and death. Those that fell ill while in a work detail would be immediately sent to the gas chambers if they did not die first.

Men selected for labour are seen more than likely being escorted to the camp's Central Sauna to be showered and re-clothed. The Central Camp Sauna, or 'bathhouse' as the SS called it, was purely designed for the mass disinfection of clothing and for the extermination of insects in clothing. The building was situated in the sector BIIg (Kanada II) near the gas chambers and Crematoria IV and V.
(USHMM/Yad Vashem)

Jewish women from Subcarpathian Rus who have been selected for forced labour are waiting to be taken to another part of the camp. *(USHMM/Yad Vashem)*

Jewish women from Subcarpathian Rus who have been selected for forced labour march towards their barracks after disinfection and head-shaving. It's more than likely that these women have been chosen for 'Kanada Kommando' duties.
(*USHMM/Yad Vashem*)

Three photographs showing Jews from Subcarpathian Rus who have been selected for forced labour and are being marched to another section of the camp.
(*USHMM/Yad Vashem*)

Following their arrival at the camp these Jewish men have been selected for labour and march towards their barracks prior to being sent to the Central Sauna. *(USHMM/Yad Vashem)*

Three photographs showing both men and women selected for labour prior to them being sent to the Central Sauna. These prisoners would be selected to perform various kinds of labour, both inside and outside the camp boundaries. There were more than forty Auschwitz sub-camps surrounding Birkenau comprising various German industrial plants and farms. Thousands of labourers were sent out to work in these sub-camps. Those that fell ill or were too weak to perform their work detail were sent to the gas chambers and murdered. *(USHMM/Yad Vashem)*

Female Jews march towards their barracks carrying bed rolls after disinfection and head-shaving. *(USHMM/Yad Vashem)*

Jewish women from Subcarpathian Rus transport who have been selected for forced labour stand at a roll-call in front of the kitchen. Note that all the females have had their heads shaved. *(USHMM/Yad Vashem)*

A large group of Jewish women from a Subcarpathian Rus transport who have been selected for forced labour wait for further processing after disinfection and head-shaving. *(USHMM/Yad Vashem)*

Selected female labourers march towards their barracks carrying bed rolls after disinfection and head-shaving. The building on the right is the kitchen of the women's camp. *(USHMM/Yad Vashem)*

(**Above**) Women prisoners from a Subcarpathian Rus transport who have been selected for forced labour march towards their barracks after disinfection, their heads shaved and a registration number tattooed on their left arm. (*USHMM/Yad Vashem*)

(**Opposite, above**) Jewish women march towards their barracks after disinfection. (*USHMM/Yad Vashem*)

(**Opposite, below**) A mass of Jewish women from a Subcarpathian Rus transport who have been selected for forced labour march towards their barracks after disinfection and head-shaving. (*USHMM/Yad Vashem*)

Two photographs showing Jewish women from a Subcarpathian Rus transport marching towards their barracks in preparation for work detail. Many of the Hungarian women that were selected for work duties between May and July 1944 were made into 'Kanada Kommandos' due to the high volume of transports arriving daily and the urgent requirement to process those that arrived. *(USHMM/Yad Vashem)*

Two photographs showing men selected for work detail. They await further processing after having been disinfected and issued with underclothing. *(USHMM/Yad Vashem)*

Chapter Five

Murder

Following the selection process, those that were destined for death were separated at the unloading ramp from those that were chosen for slave labour. Age was one of the principal criteria for selection. All children below the age of 14 and the elderly were sent to die. Trucks were parked near the selection area to transport those too unwell to walk to the crematoria, while the rest marched. Long columns of people that were selected for 'processing' were walked down to the bottom of Birkenau to await their fate. Hundreds of Hungarian Jews huddled together, often mothers carrying their young children or leading them by the hand, making their way to the crematoria.

All through the procedure the victims were told calmly that they were to bathe and be deloused. Jews under the supervision of the *Sonderkommando* were ordered to undress, and kindly requested to keep their personal effects together for when they returned. They were then led naked in file down the crematorium stairway with its metal guard rails to the basement through a doorway with a sign that read 'Bath and Disinfection Room'. As they entered the room they could see that from the ceiling hung sieves mounted on pieces of wood or metal, which appeared to be shower heads. Once crammed inside, the airtight door to the room was slammed shut and secured by two latch bars, which were screwed tight. So that the killing process could be observed, there was a specially-designed peephole consisting of a double pane of glass. Through this opening the SS watched as 1.0 or 1.5kg of pale blue-green granulated Zyklon B (a cyanide-based pesticide) was poured in from the roof by SS medical orderlies wearing gas masks. It entered the room via four metal meshed hollow columns that protruded from the concrete ceiling. When the gas was dropped into the room the victims started screaming and panicking, but their death agonies were not heard for long because the Zyklon B used was forty times the lethal dose. In a few minutes – five at most – the gas chamber fell silent. Once they were sure that all the victims were no longer moving, the air extraction system was then switched on for at least twenty or thirty minutes so that it could suck out the poisoned air that was still in the chamber. The gas-tight door was then unbolted and opened, and the gruesome task of extracting the dead women, children and old people was begun immediately by the *Sonderkommando*.

During the gassing procedure, SS surgeons on duty in the camp regularly waited nearby with an SS hospital orderly with an oxygen apparatus to revive SS men in case any of them should succumb to the poisonous fumes. Once they were certain that all inside were dead, the doors and the windows were opened to ventilate the rooms.

Höss and some of his SS personnel regularly watched the shipments arrive and became morbidly fascinated by the spectacle. Yet the demands placed on the camps' killing apparatus were causing a logistical nightmare for Höss. On 21 May, just three days after the first shipment arrived at Birkenau, both the incinerators of Crematoria II and III were shut down and had to be serviced. Consequently victims from the transports that day were disposed of in the three incineration ditches next to Crematorium V. Though the specially-built track from the crematorium to the pits had been laid it was never used because it was considered an inconvenience. Instead the *Sonderkommando* had to drag the corpses directly from the gas chamber to the pits. The corpse disposal process was required to be undertaken quickly and efficiently in order to make way for the next train arrivals. In fact, within a period of just two weeks approximately 122,700 persons that were deemed unsuitable for forced labour were subsequently sent to their death. Birkenau was effectively gassing more than 8,000 Jews on average each day. For the Auschwitz authorities the numbers were no less impressive for it was the most sustained mass killing so far in the history of the camp and only comparable to the scale of murders undertaken at Treblinka during July and August 1942.

In order to ensure that the camp would not degenerate into chaotic disorder, Höss increased the numbers of *Sonderkommando* that were working in shifts in the four crematoria. By the end of May there were almost 900 of these people living and working in the crematoria. The whole of this horrific operation was supervised by only a handful of SS men. The sight of women and children going to their deaths had become such a common feature at Auschwitz that very often these SS men would stand around, chatting and joking among themselves. Many of them had become so hardened to the brutality of overseeing the killings that there were no reports ever filed of any SS personnel having any kind of psychological breakdown.

The systematic murder of the Hungarian Jews in the summer months of 1944 evolved into its newest and deadliest phase yet. Throughout June more trains continued to arrive from Hungary. Although the operation was a success, the high numbers gassed began to exceed the incineration capacity, resulting in the crematoria overflowing with the dead. Many victims were already being burned in the pits nearby to cope with the high number of corpses, but *SS-Hauptscharführer* Otto Moll, who oversaw the liquidation of the Hungarian Jews, assured his superiors that the 'Moll Plan' would be achieved swiftly and successfully. Moll was put in charge of all the crematoria at the camp and it was he who organized the large-scale extermination of the people arriving in the Hungarian convoys. Prior to the first shipments it was Moll who ordered pits to be dug alongside Crematorium V and restarted the activity of Bunker 2, which had been lying idle, and its pits. Each pit was dug in the vicinity of the gas chambers for the burning of large numbers of corpses that the crematoria would be unable to cope with. In fact, at the height of the Hungarian arrivals nine such pits were dug. Each of them was huge: almost 50m long, 8m wide and 2m deep. At the bottom of each pit a channel was dug in order to collect body fat from the burning corpses. This fat was used for fuel and to keep the bodies burning.

Over the coming weeks the orgy of destruction escalated. Thousands of Hungarian Jews continued their one-way passage to the crematoria, including valuable labour. Höss had observed how families had often fought to stay together during the selections and watched with fascination how children clung to their mothers, screaming and crying. Instead of wrenching children from their mothers' arms he had learned that the best way to prevent any emotional disturbances was to reluctantly send young healthy women suitable for hard labour to the gas chambers with their offspring. Many Hungarian women and children went to their deaths in this way.

No matter how gruesome the outcome was for these hapless Hungarian Jews during the summer of 1944, Höss had created the perfect killing factory on an industrial scale. All four crematoria were now working more or less on a daily basis, killing thousands each day. The ovens continued to work at full capacity and the incineration ditches were being used day and night. The frenetic gassings and burnings carried on for days and weeks, regardless of the deteriorating military situation. During July an average of 3,500 people per day were arriving at the ramps with more than three-quarters of the new arrivals being sent directly to the crematoria for 'special treatment'. This phenomenal figure certainly demonstrated Höss's efficiency to oversee *Aktion Höss* with a fanatical determination. In no less than eight weeks he had masterminded the killing of more than 320,000 Hungarian Jews. The numbers were truly impressive to the Nazis, but reports from Budapest confirmed that the deportations were to be suspended. By the end of July with the number of transports dwindling, the Hungarian operation ended. Just before Höss left Auschwitz on 29 July and returned to Berlin, Baer was given command of the garrison. Höss knew that Auschwitz had finally evolved, and it was now left in the capable hands of the new commander to start making plans to liquidate whole sections of Birkenau. One particular section that had been discussed before Höss's departure was the gypsy camp. At its peak there were estimated to be some 23,000 gypsy men and women in the camp. However, thanks to overcrowding combined with a lack of food and water, disease had quickly spread, killing 20,000 of the 23,000 gypsies. Those remaining were rounded up on the night of 2 August and marched off to the crematoria and gassed. Höss was not present at the liquidation, but he was informed by *SS-Untersturmführer* Johann Schwarzhuber, who was *Lagerführer* of the men's camp at Birkenau, that it had not been an easy task gassing them as many had suddenly realized their fate.

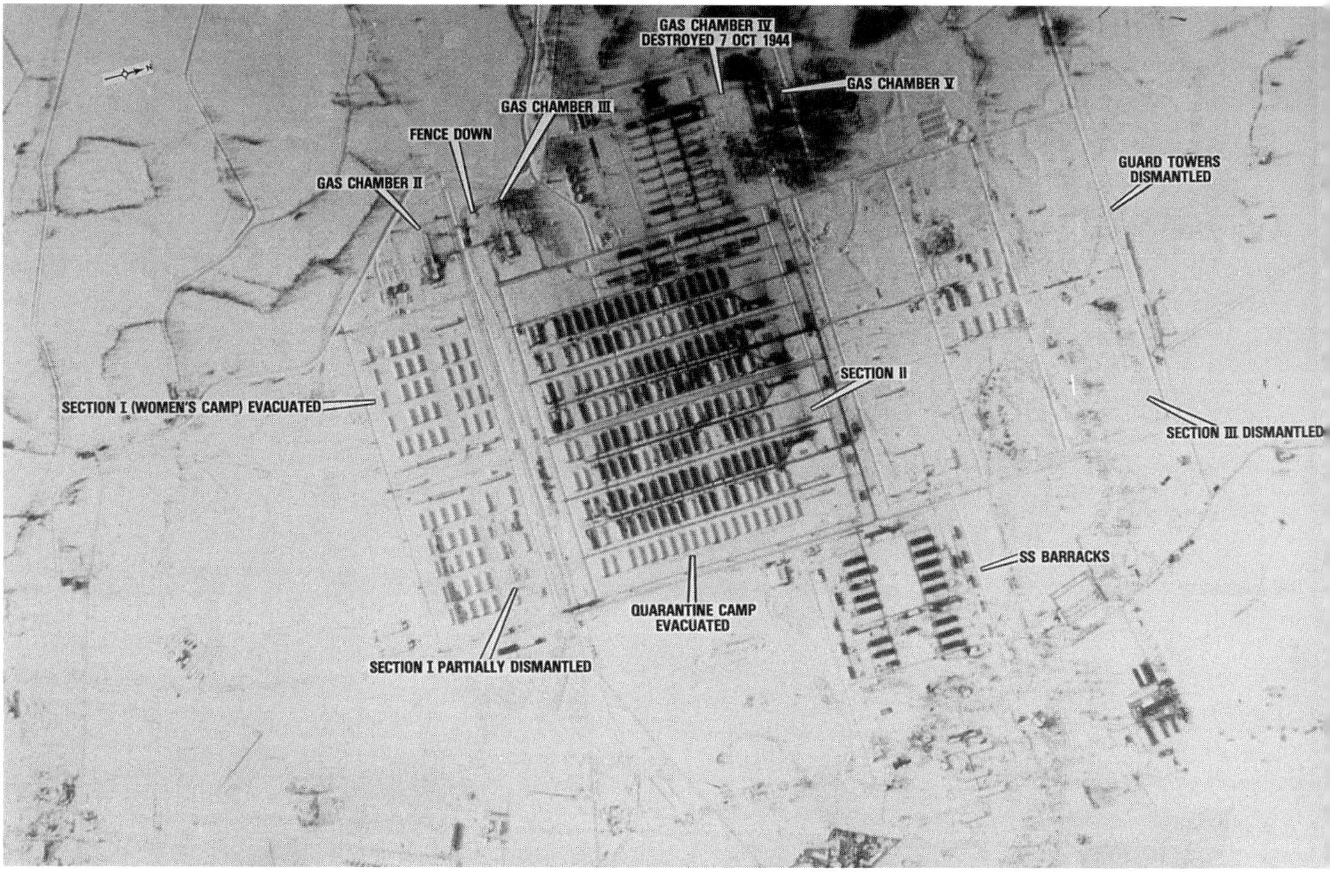

Top image labels

- GAS CHAMBER IV DESTROYED 7 OCT 1944
- GAS CHAMBER V
- GAS CHAMBER III
- FENCE DOWN
- GAS CHAMBER II
- GUARD TOWERS DISMANTLED
- SECTION I (WOMEN'S CAMP) EVACUATED
- SECTION II
- SECTION III DISMANTLED
- SS BARRACKS
- SECTION I PARTIALLY DISMANTLED
- QUARANTINE CAMP EVACUATED

Bottom image labels

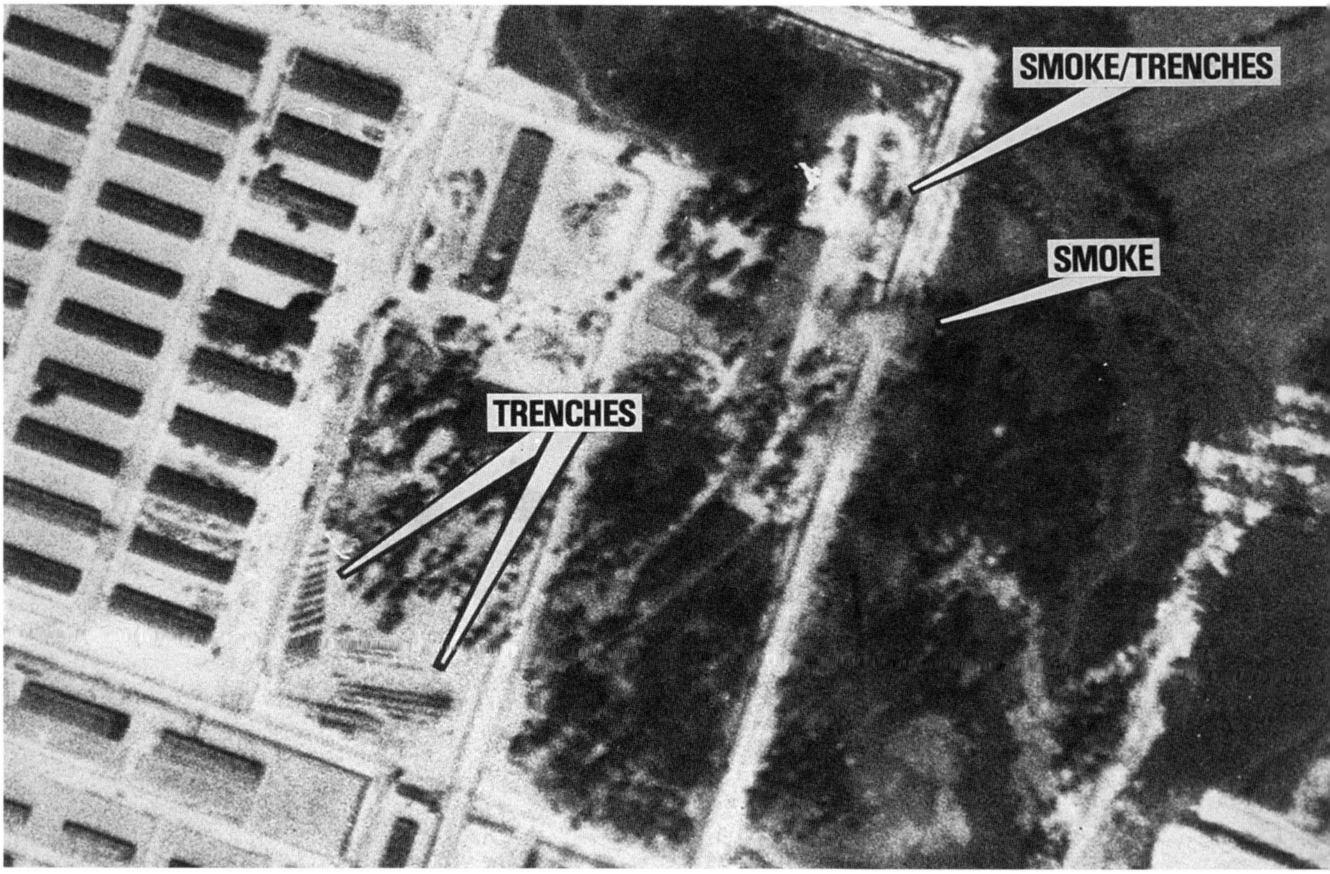

- SMOKE/TRENCHES
- SMOKE
- TRENCHES

Three photographs taken by Allied aircraft during a series of reconnaissance missions over Birkenau from 4 April 1944 to 14 January 1945. It should be noted that the photo analysts never realized the significance of Birkenau as a death camp until after its liberation in January 1945. The reconnaissance photo taken on 25 August 1944 clearly shows Crematoria II and III, the prisoners' wooden barracks, prisoners and a train. (*Auschwitz-Birkenau Museum/NARA*)

SS-Hauptsturmführer Otto Moll was in charge of all four crematoria. Often dressed in a special white protective suit with a gas mask, he was regularly seen throwing the saturated Zyklon B pellets through a little vent in the roof of the gas chambers.

The first of three photographs showing Jewish men from Subcarpathian Rus who are waiting to be sent to the gas chamber. *(USHMM/Yad Vashem)*

(**Opposite, above**) Mothers with their children have been selected for death. They appear to be at the bottom of the service road walking towards Crematorium II. (*USHMM/Yad Vashem*)

(**Opposite, below**) Jewish men who have been selected for death are directed along the service road towards Crematoria II and III. The majority of Jews that arrived through the gates of Birkenau were immediately sent to their death. There were roughly 3,300 people per day arriving and sometimes that figure even rose to 4,300. On 20 May, for instance, one convoy arrived with an average of 3,000 people, of whom some 1,000 were able and 2,000 were unable to work. The following day on 21 May two convoys were reported to have arrived from Hungary with 6,000 people, of whom 2,000 were able to work and the remainder were directly sent to their deaths. During that day the incinerators of both Crematoria II and III were being serviced so the victims from the transport were disposed of in the three incineration ditches next to Crematorium V. (*USHMM/Yad Vashem*)

(**Above**) Jewish women and their children have just been selected for death and prepare to walk along the service road towards the gas chambers. (*USHMM/Yad Vashem*)

Jewish women assist a frail old woman towards the service road following their selection for death.
(USHMM/Yad Vashem)

Five photographs showing Jewish women and children from Subcarpathian Rus who have been selected for death walking towards the gas chambers. (USHMM/Yad Vashem)

93

Old men from a newly-arrived transport have been selected for death and walk towards the gas chambers. *(USHMM/Yad Vashem)*

Three photographs showing mothers with their children and probably grandparents selected for death. Throughout the process of selection the SS tried to maintain an element of calm in order to reduce panic among the Jews. It was for this reason that they decided to reluctantly send perfectly fit mothers to the gas chambers in order to soothe their offspring as they were led into the changing rooms. *(USHMM/Yad Vashem)*

The first of fifteen photographs showing Subcarpathian Rus people who have been selected for death waiting in a clearing near a grove of trees before being led to the gas chambers. This series of photographs was taken near Crematoria IV and V. Although the 'Hungarian action' was the most sustained mass killing so far in the history of the Auschwitz camp and was comparable to the scale of murders carried out at Treblinka during July and August 1942, it was also the most problematic for the murderers. There were so many Jews that had been selected to die that frequently hundreds of women and children, including the old, had to sit and wait for some considerable time outside the compound of the crematoria before being ordered to undress and be led through the crematoria to their deaths.
(USHMM/Yad-Vashem Museum)

Mothers with their children have been selected for death and await their fate. One mother appears to be smiling, obviously with no idea that she and her family will soon be murdered. They are under the impression that they are waiting to be showered and disinfected before rejoining their family and friends. Within a period of just two weeks in May approximately 122,700 persons that were deemed unsuitable for forced labour were subsequently sent to their deaths. Birkenau was effectively gassing more than 8,000 Jews on average each day. *(USHMM/Yad Vashem)*

(**Above**) Jewish women and children from Subcarpathian Rus who have been selected for death walk towards the gas chambers. Crematorium III can be seen behind them. By the end of June Birkenau had an official daily incineration output of some 4,756 corpses. Yet, despite frequent requests by the engineers not to overload the crematoria, the Auschwitz authorities continued to operate the installations at their absolute limit. According to reports the furnaces were not being operated correctly, were being constantly overheated, and it was suggested that the *Sonderkommando* were deliberately damaging the internal lining with their fire irons. By early July the transports to Birkenau had become much larger and the numbers of people selected for death increased massively.

(**Opposite & overleaf**) Five clandestine photos taken in Auschwitz-Birkenau showing two naked women running before being executed, and others showing the *Sonderkommando* burning bodies. The photographer clearly had no time to aim the camera properly as he was afraid of being caught. Consequently he just pressed the shutter without aiming and without looking. It's probable that these photos were taken in the summer of 1944 during the 'Hungarian operation'. Open-air burning procedures like this were not uncommon at the camp. Due to the high numbers gassed at the camp the crematoria often exceeded their official incineration capacity, and as a result they began overflowing with the dead. These two photos are part of a series taken by an inmate called Alex, and it was members of the *Sonderkommando* in the camp's Crematorium V that helped to obtain and hide the camera and act as lookouts. (*Auschwitz-Birkenau Museum*)

A photograph of Crematorium IV taken in summer 1943. The gas chambers are located in the lower wing (left) of the building. At the end of June 1944, owing to the increased demand for cremations, a *Sonderkommando* team was moved from their barracks to live in Crematoria II, III and IV. *(Auschwitz-Birkenau State Museum)*

Crematorium III. This gassing facility functioned from June 1943 to November 1944. According to calculations by the German authorities, 1,440 corpses could be burned in this crematorium every twenty-four hours. However, it is estimated from the testimonies of former prisoners that this figure could be higher. *(Auschwitz-Birkenau State Museum)*

Chapter Six

The Aftermath

Following the deportation of some 438,000 Hungarian Jews to Auschwitz-Birkenau, it is reported that only 10 per cent were selected for slave labour and the remainder were all murdered in the gas chambers. The SS looked upon these numbers as truly impressive, but reports from Budapest confirmed that the deportations were to be suspended. By the end of July, with the number of transports in Birkenau dwindling, Operation HÖSS finally ended. Just before Höss left Auschwitz on 29 July and returned to Berlin, he attended a farewell party with his associates at the camp's retreat at Solahütte. Along with Josef Kramer, Höcker, Baer, Otto Moll (the supervisor of the gas chambers), Franz Hössler, Dr Josef Mengele (who had selected 'specimens' for his medical experiments from among the newly-arrived transports of Hungarian Jews) and other officers and personnel, they spent the afternoon enjoying time together laughing, joking and gossiping.

Höss made it known that he had effectively done an exceptional job in processing the Hungarian Jews. Although the operation was now at its end, the fate of the remaining Jews in Hungary was not over. In Budapest, the Jews there had survived two deportation attempts to Auschwitz in early July during the Höss action and late August. However, by late September preparations were still being made by Eichmann to transport the remaining Jews to Auschwitz. Even as the Soviet army approached Hungary and plans were being made to fortify the city against a Russian attack, the SS were determined 'to clear the last vestiges of Jewry from Hungarian soil'. The new Hungarian government under the control of Ferenc Szálasi, the leader of the fascist and radically anti-Semitic Arrow Cross Party, was more than willing to assist his SS counterparts. Through October and November the Arrow Cross Party unleashed a reign of terror against the Jews. Hundreds were murdered, and those that escaped from death were rounded up and either incarcerated into a ghetto in preparation for their deportation, mobilized to construct anti-tank defences or force-marched to the Austrian border for slave labour.

44-Hütte Soletal

(**Opposite, above**) A view from above of a building and surrounding grounds of Solahütte, the SS retreat outside Auschwitz. This rustic SS getaway facility was used on 29 July 1944 in honour of Rudolf Höss who completed his tenure as garrison senior. The party gathering on this date also earmarked the completion of the destruction of the Hungarian Jews at Birkenau. In attendance were some of the most notorious officers of the concentration camp system. (*USHMM*)

(**Opposite, below**) Standing in front of the building in Solahütte facing the camera, second from left, is Karl Höcker. Next to him is *SS-Obersturmführer* Max Sell, between 1943 and 1945 first *Arbeitseinsatzführer* in Auschwitz and afterwards in Mittelbau-Dora. (*USHMM*)

(**Above**) Pictured on the far left is Josef Kramer (back to camera) and Dr Josef Mengele, Commandant Richard Baer, his adjutant Karl Höcker and Walter Schmidetzki. (*USHMM*)

(**Above**) Pictured on the far left is Dr Josef Mengele. On the right are Commandant Richard Baer and his adjutant Karl Höcker. (USHMM)

(**Opposite, above**) From left to right: Richard Baer (commandant of Auschwitz), Karl Höcker (his adjutant), and Rudolf Höss (the former commandant). (USHMM)

(**Opposite, below**) From left to right: Richard Baer, Dr Josef Mengele and Rudolf Höss. (USHMM)

From left to right: Josef Kramer, Dr Josef Mengele, Richard Baer, Karl Höcker and Walter Schmidetzki. (*USHMM*)

From left to right: Josef Kramer, Anton Thumann, Karl Höcker and Franz Hössler. (*USHMM*)

From left to right: Rudolf Höss, Josef Kramer (partially obscured behind him), Anton Thumann and Karl Höcker. (USHMM)

Left to right: Richard Baer, Josef Mengele, Josef Kramer, Rudolf Höss and Anton Thumann. (USHMM)

Appendix I

Timeline

Prior to Rudolf Höss's return to Auschwitz, the Director of Section IV-B4 of the RSHA, SS Adolf Eichmann, begins plans for the destruction of the Hungarian Jews. He outlines a number of issues during a visit to Auschwitz, including the shutting down of Incineration Facility V, which meant that corpses were being incinerated in outdoor pits near old Bunker 2. He also catalogues the delay in the construction of a three-track railway spur from the unloading ramp to Auschwitz II.

As plans get under way for the implementation of the arrival of the Hungarian Jews Eichmann requests to the RSHA that Höss is appointed director for the operation of destroying the Hungarian Jews. He is also given responsibility for training the new Commandant SS Richard Baer, who is taking over from Liebehenschel, and SS Captain Josef Kramer, who replaces Hartjenstein as Commandant of Auschwitz.

For the Hungarian operation Eichmann outlines to Höss in early May 1944 plans to send four transports of Hungarian Jews per day to their destruction in Auschwitz. However, due to the lack of facilities at the camp for killing so many Jews over a short period of time, Höss is compelled to travel to Budapest, where he meets railway officials. They agree that on alternate days two trains of deportees, then three trains, should be dispatched. The agreement with railway officials in Budapest provides for a total of 111 trains.

With the arrival of the first transports of deported Hungarian Jews, Eichmann arrives at Birkenau for an inspection of the extermination facilities to ensure it will be run properly as Himmler is demanding a mass acceleration of the so-called Hungary Operation. The destruction of the Hungarian Jews is given the name Operation HÖSS. To conceal the steadily growing number of prisoners who are selected from the transports for destruction, the SS introduces two new series of numerals for Jewish prisoners beginning with A-1, one each for men and women, and later a series beginning with B-1 for men only.

It is agreed that from the mass transports of Hungarian Jews only the young, healthy and strong Jews of both sexes are selected for work detail. Due to the workload of selection, the prisoners for labour will not be recorded in the camp registers. They are accommodated in Camp B-IIc, where young, able-bodied female Jews are kept. In the old Gypsy Family Camp B-IIe, young, able-bodied male and female Jewish prisoners are to be accommodated. Camp B-IIb, which was the Theresienstadt Family Camp, and Section B-III, which is still under construction and known as 'Mexico', were to receive female prisoners. The Jews temporarily located in Birkenau receive no identification numbers and are not tattooed.

The selection process was conducted at exact intervals. When the camp administration has a need for labourers, it sends some prisoners from these camps to specific auxiliary camps or to the labour squads. Then they are registered and given numbers. Under the direction of the WVHA, others are transferred to armaments plants in the interior of the Reich.

13 March. The Degesch Company submits an invoice for 1,050 RM for the delivery of 462lb of the gas Zyklon B to Auschwitz on 8 March.

25 April. The Special Squad that operates the four crematoria and gas chambers totals 207 prisoners.

2 May. Two transports arrive from Hungary: the first sent from Budapest on 29 April and containing approximately 1,800 able-bodied Jewish men and women between the ages of 16 and 50; the second sent on 30 April from Topolya containing 2,000 able-bodied prisoners. After the selection 486 men were given numbers 186645–187130 and 616 women were given numbers 76385–76459 and 80000–80540 and are admitted to the camp. The remaining 2,698 men and women are killed in the gas chambers.

4 May. At a conference in Vienna a travel plan is agreed for the deportation transports of Jews from Hungary. These comprise 10 camps in the Carpathia area (Zone 1) with approximately 200,000 Jews from the Siebenbergen area (Zone II), where approximately 110,000 Jews were located. It is decided that in mid-May four transports, each with 3,000 persons, should take place daily. The conclusion of the deportations from these zones is estimated to be completed within a month.

8 May. The function of the SS Camp Senior is taken over until further notice by the Head of Office D-I in the WVHA, the former Commandant SS Rudolf Höss.

9 May. With plans for the acceleration of the destruction of the Hungarian Jews, Höss announces a series of directives. He orders that the expansion of the platform and the three-track rail connection in Birkenau be sped up. He also instructs that the inactive cremation ovens in Crematorium V be put in operation. Next to the crematoria he orders gangs to dig five crematoria pits (three large and two smaller ones). This will be used for the incineration of corpses. He also orders that Bunker 2 is to be put back into operation and incineration trenches are to be dug nearby. Barracks were to be constructed for use as changing rooms. Höss promotes the commander of Gleiwitz I, SS Otto Moll, as director of all crematoria.

15 May. The number of prisoners in the Special Squad is increased by 100. A total of 308 prisoners are now employed in the Special Squad.

16 May. Three freight trains arrive on the new track connection at Birkenau comprising the first transports of Hungarian Jews. The Jews are ordered to unload their luggage and to stand in rows of five. They are selected and those unfit for work are led in the direction of the crematoria. Smoke from the crematoria chimneys begins to rise.

25 May. Number of Hungarian Jews killed is estimated at over 100,000 people and the work shifts of the SS men involved in the extermination operation is forty-eight uninterrupted hours, followed by an eight-hour break. The German ambassador and plenipotentiary for Hungary, SS Dr Edmund Veesenmayer, informs the Foreign Ministry that as of 25 May nearly 150,000 Jews have been deported from Zone I (Carpathia) and Zone II (Siebenbergen) in Hungary to the target area and that the transports from Zone III, the area north of Budapest, should take place 11–16 June and should involve approximately 65,000 Jews. Every night eight trains arrive; every day five. The trains consist of 48–50 cars each, and in each car are 100 people.

31 May. The management of the crematoria in Auschwitz II orders four shovels 8 × 10 inches for shovelling coke into the generators, and five cast-steel frames including the complete wooden model for the iron shield plates. The management of the Birkenau crematoria gives the contract to make small repairs on shovels and pokers and to weld two large and five small oven doors and an iron plate.

3 June. In connection with the repeated break-outs from the crematorium buildings by Hungarian Jews, the practice of turning off the current in the electric fence in the daytime is discontinued. The electrical current is left on.

13 June. The Reich's plenipotentiary in Hungary, Dr Veesenmayer, notifies the Foreign Ministry that the deportation of Jews from the areas of Carpathia and Siebenbergen (Zones I and II) has been completed on 7 June. A total of 289,357 Jews have been deported to the 'target destination' in ninety-two trains, each of which consisted of forty-five cars. The concentration of Jews from the area north of Budapest (Zone III) was completed on 10 June. The transports are planned for 11–16 June and 21 trains. The anticipated total is approximately 67,000 deportees. It is planned to complete the concentration of Jews in Zone IV, east of the Donau [Danube] except for Budapest, by 24 June. The deportation of the nearly 45,000 Jews would take place on 25–28 June.

17 June. Dr Veesenmayer reports in a telegram to Foreign Minister von Ribbentrop that as of 17 June nearly 340,000 Jews have been deported from Hungary to the Reich territory. This number could be doubled by the end of July, according to the current estimates, without producing increased traffic congestion, and later a total of approximately 900,000 could be reached.

26 June. The management of the crematoria in Auschwitz II receives four sieves for sifting human ashes. The sieves, ordered on 7 June, will serve to sift out the unburned human bones which were taken out of the incineration trenches near the crematoria and ground in special mortars. The sieves cost 232 RM.

10 July. The St. Gallen newspaper *Die Ostschweiz* (*Eastern Switzerland*) publishes an article with the title 'People are Disappearing'. The article states that so far approximately 400,000 Hungarian Jews have been deported to Poland, of whom the majority have been sent to Auschwitz. The deportations, it continues, began on 15 May when sixty-two cars with Jewish children arrived in Poland. Since then it has been observed that daily six trains of Jews pass the train station in Płaszów near Kraków, whereby the majority are taken to Auschwitz and the people are killed in the gas chambers. According to reports these gas chambers have a daily capacity of 6,000 persons.

11 July. Dr Veesenmayer reports in a telegram to the Foreign Minister of the Third Reich that the deportation of 55,741 Jews from Zone V (the area west of the Danube in the suburbs of Budapest) was completed on 9 July. The number of Jews deported from all five zones in Hungary reaches 437,402 persons.

15 July. The camp resistance organization states in its report to Kraków: 'From 13 June on there was a several day pause in the transports of Hungarian Jews. Between 16 May and 13 June over 300,000 Hungarian Jews were delivered on 113 trains. In addition there was a transport of French Jews (2,500), a transport of Italian Jews (1,500), two transports of Czech Jews (50) headed by the elder of the Czech ghetto, who was immediately gassed with his entire family. In addition to these numbers there were 100 English and American citizens of Jewish descent delivered, who were separated and destroyed in particular ways … The evacuation of Poles and Russians as the most dangerous elements of the camp continues. 4,500 prisoners, among them 2,900 Poles and 1,600 Russians, were evacuated in June in three transports from Auschwitz I.'

29 July. SS Lieutenant Colonel Höss, authorized to annihilate the Hungarian Jews, leaves Auschwitz. Commandant Richard Baer of Auschwitz I becomes SS Camp Senior. 873 prisoners, among them three skilled workers, work in the so-called Special Squad operating the gas chambers, the four crematoria and the incineration pits in day and night shifts.

(Excerpts taken from Czech, Danuta, *Auschwitz Chronicle 1939–1945: From the Archives of the Auschwitz Memorial and the German Federal Archives*, 1989.)

Appendix II

Hungarian Jewish ghettos

The following is a list of Hungarian Jewish ghettos from which the Jews were removed and transported to Auschwitz-Birkenau:

1. Sopron
2. Szombathely
3. Sárvár
4. Nagykanizsa
5. Pápa
6. Dunajska Streda (Dunaszerdahe)
7. Barcs
8. Györ
9. Kaposvár
10. Nove Zamky (Érsekújvár)
11. Komárno (Komárom)
12. Pécs
13. Szekesfehervár
14. Levice (Léva)
15. Paks
16. Baja
17. Óbuda
18. Budakalasz
19. Békesmegyer
20. Szásrégen
21. Balassagyarmat
22. Kistarcsa
23. Rákoscaba
24. Bacsalmás
25. Monor
26. Bačka Topola
27. Keckscemét
28. Salgotarján
29. Szeged
30. Szolnok
31. Diosgyör
32. Miskolc
33. Békescsaba
34. Košice (Kassa)
35. Sátoraljaujhely
36. Nyiregyháza
37. Oradea (Nagyvárod)
38. Kisvárda
39. Užhorod (Ungwar)
40. Mátészalka
41. Mukačevo (Munkács)
42. Berehovo (Beregszász)
43. Simleu Silvaniei (Szilágysomló)
44. Satu Mare (Szatmámémeti)
45. Vynohradiv (Nagyszöllös)
45. Chust (Huszt)
46. Tačev (Técsö)
47. Baja Mare (Nagybánya)
49. Cluj Napoca (Kolozsvár)
50. Okormezo (Ökörmezö)
51. Solotvina (Aknaszlatina)
52. Sighetu Marmatiei (Mármarossziget)
53. Dej (Dés)
54. Viseu de Sus (Felsövisó)
55. Bistrita (Beszterce)
56. Tirgu Mures (Márosvásárhely)

Appendix III

Kassa List

Over a period of 56 days, some 437,402 Jews were deported from Hungary in 147 trains. The majority of the transports were handed over by the Hungarian authorities to the Germans at Kassa. The head of the Kassa railway station collected the data of the trains passing through the station. According to the Kassa list, the Germans transported more than 400,426 Jews in 137 trains from the Hungarian gendarmes at Kassa.

Place	Date	Number	Place	Date	Number
Nyíregyháza	May 14.	3,200	Nyíregyháza	May 21.	3,274
Nyíregyháza	May 14.	3,200	Sátoraljaújhely	May 21.	3,290
Munkács	May 14.	3,169	Munkács	May 21.	2,861
Kassa	May 16.	3,055	Máramarossziget	May 22.	3,490
Beregszász	May 16.	3,818	Ungvár	May 22.	3,335
Máramarossziget	May 16.	3,007	Szatmárnémeti	May 22.	3,300
Munkács	May 16.	3,629	Mátészalka	May 22.	3,298
Kassa	May 16.	3,629	Felsővisó	May 23.	3,023
Kassa	May 17.	3,352	Nyíregyháza	May 23.	3,272
Ungvár	May 17.	3,455	Munkács	May 23.	3,269
Ökörmező	May 17.	3,052	Nagyvárad	May 23.	3,110
Munkács	May 17.	3,306	Beregszász	May 24.	2,602
Máramarossziget	May 18.	3,248	Kassa	May 24.	3,172
Beregszász	May 18.	3,569	Huszt	May 24.	3,328
Sátoraljaújhely	May 18.	3,439	Munkács	May 24.	3,080
Munkács	May 18.	3,025	Ungvár	May 25.	3,334
Felsővisó	May 19.	3,032	Nagyvárad	May 25.	3,148
Mátészalka	May 19.	3,299	Kolozsvár	May 25.	3,130
Szatmárnémeti	May 19.	3,000	Aknaszlatina	May 25.	3,317
Munkács	May 19.	3,222	Felsővisó	May 25.	3,006
Máramarossziget	May 20.	3,104	Huszt	May 26.	3,249
Nagyszőllős	May 20.	3,458	Szatmárnémeti	May 26.	3,336
Munkács	May 20.	3,026	Sátoraljaújhely	May 27.	3,325
Felsővisó	May 21.	3,013	Nagyszőllős	May 27.	3,415

Nyíregyháza	May 27.	2,708	Dés	June 8.	1,364
Ungvár	May 27.	2,988	Kolozsvár	June 8.	1,784
Marosvásárhely	May 27.	3,183	Marosvásárhely	June 8.	1,163
Técső	May 28.	2,208	Kolozsvár	June 9.	1,447
Dés	May 28.	3,150	Maklár	June 11.	2,794
Nagyvárad	May 28.	3,227	Diósgyőr	June 12.	2,675
Beregszász	May 29.	860	Balassagyarmat	June 12.	2,810
Mátészalka	May 29.	3,299	Diósgyőr	June 12.	2,941
Kolozsvár	May 29.	3,417	Érsekújvár	June 12.	2,899
Szatmárnémeti	May 29.	3,306	Diósgyőr	June 12.	3,051
Nagyvárad	May 29.	3,166	Hatvan	June 13.	2,961
Kisvárda	May 30.	3,475	Komárom	June 13.	2,790
Marosvásárhely	May 30.	3,203	Salgótarján	June 13.	2,310
Nagyvárad	May 30.	3,187	Miskolc - Diósgyőr	June 14.	3,968
Szatmárnémeti	May 30.	3,300	Balassagyarmat	June 14.	1,867
Ungvár	May 31.	3,056	Léva	June 15.	2,678
Kolozsvár	May 31.	3,270	Miskolc	June 15.	2,829
Nagybánya	May 31.	3,073	Érsekújvár	June 15.	1,980
Szilágysomlyó	May 31.	3,106	Győr	June 16.	2,985
Mátészalka	June 1.	3,299	Komárom	June 16.	2,673
Kisvárda	June 1.	3,421	Dunaszerdahely	June 16.	2,969
Nagyvárad	June 1.	3,059	Debrecen	June 25.	2,286
Szatmárnémeti	June 1.	2,615	Szeged	June 26.	3,199
Huszt	June 2.	2,396	Debrecen	June 27.	3,842
Beszterce	June 2.	3,106	Kecskemét	June 27.	2,642
Kolozsvár	June 2.	3,100	Nagyvárad	June 27.	2,819
Nagyszőllős	June 3.	2,967	Békéscsaba	June 27.	3,118
Kassa	June 3.	2,499	Bácsalmás	June 28.	2,737
Nagyvárad	June 3.	2,972	Kecskemét	June 29.	2,790
Szilágysomlyó	June 3.	3,161	Szolnok	June 29.	2,038
Szászrégen	June 4.	3,149	Debrecen	June 29.	3,026
Sátoraljaújhely	June 4.	2,567	Sárvár	July 5.	3,105
Nagyvárad	June 5.	2,527	Szombathely	July 5.	3,103
Mátészalka	June 5.	3,100	Kaposvár	July 6.	3,050
Nyíregyháza	June 5.	2,253	Pécs	July 6.	3,100
Nagybánya	June 5.	2,844	Kaposvár	July 6.	2,066
Huszt	June 6.	1,852	Sopron	July 7.	3,077
Dés	June 6.	3,160	Pápa	July 7.	2,793
Beszterce	June 6.	2,875	Paks	July 7.	1,072
Szilágysomlyó	June 6.	1,581	Monor	July 7.	3,549

Óbuda	July 7.	3,151	Óbuda	July 9.	3,072
Sárvár	July 7.	2,204	Budakalász	July 9.	3,072
Pécs	July 8.	2,523	Monor	July 9.	3,079
Óbuda	July 8.	2,997	Békásmegyer	July 9.	1,924
Monor	July 9.	3,065	Rákoscsaba	July 20.	1,230

Appendix IV

Hungarians Deported and Selected for Labour

The following table shows the number of Hungarian Jews deported to Auschwitz who were not gassed on arrival but were selected as fit for work and temporarily spared. It is estimated that some 52,752 Hungarians were designated for labour during the Höss operation.

Month	Day	Quantity of deportees	Total monthly sum	Hungarian action transport nos (16.5–11.7)	Month	Day	Quantity of deportees	Total monthly sum	Hungarian action transport nos (16.5–11.7)
May	16	221		1		"	515		32
	"	173		2		"	528		33
	17	247		3		"	529		34
	18	309		4		"	510		35
	"	441		5		26	551		36
	"	484		6		"	485		37
	"	33		7		"	674		38
	19	581"		8		"	509		39
	"	468		9		"	500		40
	"	507		10		27	528		41
	20	503		11		"	606		42
	"	647		12		"	520		43
	"	992		13		"	635		44
	21	412		14		"	441		45
	"	127		15		28	479		46
	"	556		16		"	625		47
	"	362		17		"	455		48
	"	395		18		"	477		49
	22	487		19		"	499		50
	"	368		20		"	282		51
	"	471		21		"	211		52
	"	575		22		"	304		53
	23	205		23		"	155		54
	"	196		24		30	506		55
	"	345		25		"	170		56
	"	575		26		"	457		57
	24	499		27		"	554		58
	"	630		28		31	538		59
	"	494		29		"	592		60
	"	470		30		"	466	27,629	61
	25	224		31	June	1	429		62

Month	Day	Quantity of deportees	Total monthly sum	Hungarian action transport nos (16.5–11.7)	Month	Day	Quantity of deportees	Total monthly sum	Hungarian action transport nos (16.5–11.7)
	"	519		63		15	172		105
	"	426		64		"	256		106
	"	696		65		"	62		107
	"	165		66		"	620		108
	2	620		67		16	53		109
	"	510		68			355		110
	"	379		69		17	195		111
	"	419		70		"	190		112
	3	576		71		"	353		113
	"	543		72		"	207		114
	"	497		73		18	405		115
	"	286		74		"	255		116
	"	443		75		27	215		117
	"	363		76		"	232		118
	"	358		77		29	236		119
	"	496		78		"	206		120
	5	441		79		"	193		121
	"	404		80		"	5		
	"	416		81		"	203	19,263	122
	"	397		82	July	1	318		123
	6	441		83		"	50		124
	"	524		84		"	339		125
	"	401		85		"	288		126
	7	376		86		"	219		127
	"	328		87		8	300		128
	"	269		88		"	209		129
	"	444		89		"	356		130
	8	405		90		"	361		131
	"	138		91		"	335		132
	9	280		92		9	259		133
	"	279		93		"	193		134
	10	166		94		"	220		135
	11	329		95		"	85		136
	12	3		96		10	248		137
	"	5		97		"	183		138
	"	84		98		"	299		139
	13	111		99		"	378		140
	"	162		100		11	426		141
	"	59		101		"	409		142
	14	208		102		22	371		
	"	66		103		"	11		
	"	389		104		"	2	5,860	

Appendix V

Detailed Listing of Male and Female Train Transports

The following table provides a detailed listing of both male and female train transports that were sent to Auschwitz-Birkenau. There are also four copies of original documents detailing the transports between May and August 1944. The trains listed show that they arrived at Auschwitz every day except for two periods of interruption. One of these was 16–25 June when the Strasshof trains started, and the other was 1–22 July when the Hungarian action was almost completed.

Resided at or transport from	Gaško List			Glaser List		This Analysis	
	Date Arr. Košice	Train No.	People arriving	Date Arr. Birkenau	Men selected	Women selected	People Killed
Kistarcsa, Budapest	29 Apr.	2	1,800, men	2 May	486		2,698
Backa Topola	30 Apr.		2,000	2 May		616	
Vencesello to Nyiregyhaza	14 May	1	3,200	16 May	221	243	2,736
Mukačevo	14 May	2	3,169	16 May	173	190	2,806
Košice	16 May	3	3,055	17 May	247	272	2,536
Sucha Bronika to Beregszasz	16 May	4	3,818	18 May	309	340	3,169
Beregszasz							
Sighetul Marmatiei	16 May	5	3,007	18 May	441	481	2,085
Mukačevo	16 May	6	3,629	18 May	484	532	2,613
Košice	16 May	7	3,629	18 May	33	36	3,560
Košice	17 May	8	3,352	19 May	581	639	2,132
Herincsen from Užhorod	17 May	9	3,455	19 May	468	515	2,472
Ökörmezö	17 May	10	3,052	19 May	507	558	1,987
Mukačevo	17 May	11	3,306	20 May	503	553	2,250
Sighetul Marmatiei	18 May	12	3,248	20 May	547	602	2,099
Balazser to Beregszasz	18 May	13	3,569	20 May	992	1,091	1,486
Satoruljaujhely	18 May	14	3,439	21 May	412	453	2,574
Mukačevo	18 May	15	3,025	21 May	127	140	2,758
Viseu de Sus	19 May	16	3,032	21 May	556	612	1,864
Noua Sulita to Mateszalka	19 May	17	3,299	21 May	362	398	2,539
Satu Mare	19 May	18	3,000	21 May	395	435	2,170
Mukačevo	19 May	19	3,222	22 May	487	536	2,199
Sighetul Marmatiei	20 May	20	3,104	22 May	368	405	2,331
Vinogradov	20 May	21	3,458	22 May	471	518	2,469
Mukačevo	20 May	22	3,028	22 May	575	633	1,820
Viseu de Sus	21 May	23	3,013	23 May	205	226	2,582
Nyiregyháza	21 May	24	3,274	23 May	196	216	2,862

	Gaško List			Glaser List		This Analysis	
Resided at or transport from	Date Arr. Košice	Train No.	People arriving	Date Arr. Birkenau	Men selected	Women selected	People Killed
Satoruljaujhely	21 May	25	3,290	23 May	345	380	2,565
Mukačevo	21 May	26	2,861	23 May	575	633	1,653
Sighetul Marmatiei	22 May	27	3,490	24 May	499	549	2,442
Satu Mare	22 May	29	3,300	24 May	630	693	1,977
Mateszalka	22 May	30	3,299	24 May	494	553	2,252
Viseu de Sus	23 May	31	3,023	24 May	470	517	2,036
Nyiregyháza	23 May	32	3,272	25 May	224	246	2,802
Mukačevo	23 May	33	3,269	25 May	515	567	2,187
Oradea (Nagyvárad)	23 May	34	3,110	25 May	528	581	2,001
Beregovo (Beregszász)	24 May	35	2,602	25 May	529	582	1,491
Užhorod (left 21 May)	22 May	28	3,335	26 May 25 May	510	561	2,264
Košice	24 May	36	3,172	26 May	551	606	2,015
Hust	24 May	37	3,328	26 May	485	534	2,309
Mukačevo	24 May	38	3,080	26 May	674	741	1,665
Possibly Barcs	24 May	38	3,160	26 May	509	660	1,991
Klodzsano from Užhorod	25 May	39	3,334	26 May	500	550	2,284
Oradea (Nagyvárad)	25 May	40	3,148	27 May	528	581	2,039
Cluj-Napoca	25 May	41	3,130	27 May	606	667	1,857
Akna-Szlatina	25 May	42	3,317	27 May	520	572	2,225
Viseu de Sus	25 May	43	3,006	27 May	635	699	1,672
Hust	26 May	44	3,249	27 May	441	485	2,323
Possibly Baja via Gänserndorf, Aust.	26 May	b	3,160	28 May	479	527	2,154
Possibly Baja (as above)	26 May	c	3,160	28 May	625	688	1,847
Satu Mare	26 May	45	3,336	28 May	455	501	2,380
Budszeentmihaly to Satoruljaujhely	27 May	46	3,325	28 May	477	525	2,323
Vinogradov	27 May	47	3,415	28 May	499	549	2,367
Nyiregyháza	27 May	48	2,708	28 May	282	310	2,416
Užhorod	27 May	49	2,988	28 May	211	232	2,545
Tirgu Mures	27 May	50	3,183	28 May	304	334	2,545
Tačev	28 May	51	2,208	28 May	155	171	1,882
Dej	28 May	52	3,150	28 May	506	557	2,087
Oradea	28 May	53	3,227	30 May	457	503	2,267
Bereggovo (last train)	29 May	54	860	30 May	170	187	503
	29 May	d	3,160	30 May	554	609	1,997
Rachovo to Mateszalka	29 May	55	3,299	31 May	538	592	2,169
Cluj-Napoca	29 May	56	3,417	31 May	592	651	2,172
Satu Mare	29 May	57	3,306	31 May	466	513	2,327
Oradea	29 May	58	3,166	1 June	429	472	2,265
Kisvárda	30 May	59	3,476	1 June	519	571	2,386
Tirgu Mures	30 May	60	3,203	1 June	426	469	2,308
Oradea	30 May	61	3,187	1 June	696	776	1,715
Satu Mare	30 May	62	3,300	1 June	165	182	2,953
Užhorod	31 May	63	3,056	2 June	620	682	1,754
Cluj-Napoca	31 May	64	3,270	2 June	510	561	2,199
Baia Mare	31 May	65	3,073	2 June	379	417	2,277
Simleu Silvaniei	31 May	66	3,106	2 June	419	461	2,419
Mateszalka	1 June	67	3,299	3 June	576	634	2,089
Kisvárda	1 June	68	3,421	3 June	543	597	2,281
Oradea	1 June	69	3,059	3 June	497	547	2,015
Satu Mare	1 June	70	2,615	3 June	286	315	2,014
Hust	2 June	71	2,396	4 June	443	487	1,466

	Gaško List			Glaser List		This Analysis	
Resided at or transport from	Date Arr. Košice	Train No.	People arriving	Date Arr. Birkenau	Men selected	Women selected	People Killed
Bistriţa	2 June	72	3,106	4 June	363	399	2,344
Cluj-Napoca	2 June	73	3,100	4 June	358	394	2,248
Vinogradov	3 June	74	2,937	4 June	496	546	1,895
Košice	3 June	75	2,499	5 June	441	485	1,573
Oradea	3 June	76	2,972	5 June	404	444	2,124
Simleu Silvaniei	3 June	77	3,161	5 June	416	458	2,287
Szászrégen	4 June	78	3,149	6 June	397	437	2,315
Satoruljaujhely	4 June	79	2,567	6 June	441	485	1,641
Oradea	5 June	80	2,527	6 June	524	576	1,427
Uhla to Mateszalka	5 June	81	3,100	6 June	401	441	2,258
Nyiregyháza	5 June	82	2,253	7 June	376	414	1,463
Baia Mare	5 June	83	2,844	7 June	328	361	2,155
Hust	6 June	84	1,852	7 June	269	296	1,287
Dej	6 June	85	3,160	7 June	444	488	2,228
Bistriţa	6 June	86	2,875	8 June	405	446	2,024
Simleu Silvaniei	8 June	87	1,584	8 June	138	152	1,294
Dej	8 June	88	1,364	9 June	280	308	776
Cluj Napoca	8 June	89	1,784	9 June	279	307	1,198
Tirgu Mures	8 June	90	1,163	10 June	166	183	814
Cluj-Napoca	9 June	91	1,447	11 June	329	362	756
Székesfehérvár	10 June	e	3,160	12 June	3	3	3,154
	11 June	f	3,160	12 June	5	6	3,149
Maklár	11 June	92	2,794	12 June	84	92	2,618
Diosgyör	12 June	93	2,675	13 June	111	122	2,442
Balassagyarmat	12 June	94	2,810	13 June	162	178	2,470
Diosgyör	12 June	95	2,941	13 June	59	65	2,817
Nové Zámky Érsekujvár	12 June	96	2,899	14 June	208	229	2,462
Diosgyör	12 June	97	3,051	14 June	66	73	2,912
Hatvan	13 June	98	2,961	14 June	389	428	2,144
Komárno	13 June	99	2,790	15 June	172	189	2,429
Salgotarján	13 June	100	2,310	15 June	256	282	1,772
Miskolc- Diosgyör	14 June	101	3,965	15 June	62	68	3,835
Balasagyarmat	14 June	102	1,867	15 June	620	682	565
Levice (Léva)	15 June	103	2,678	16 June	53	58	2,567
Miskolc	15 June	104	2,829	16 June	355	391	2,083
Nové ZámkyÉrsekujvár	15 June	105	1,980	17 June	195	215	1,570
Györ	16 June	106	2,985	17 June	190	209	2,586
Komárno (Komárom)	16 June	107	2,673	17 June	353	388	1,932
Dunajska Streda Dunaszerdahely	16 June	108	2,969	17 June	207	228	2,534
	17 June	g	3,160	18 June	405	446	2,309
Debrecen	25 June	109	3,006	26 June	255	281	2,470
Szeged	26 June	110	3,199	27 June	215	237	2,747
Debrecen	27 June	111	3,842	28 June	2	2	3,838
Kecsemét	27 June	112	2,642	29 June	232	255	2,155
Békéscsaba	27 June	114	3,118	29 June	236	260	2,622
From Serretyudveri to Oradea (Nagyvárad) (left ghetto 26 June)	27 June	113	2,819	29 June	206	227	2,386
Bácsalmás	28 June	115	3,737	29 June	193	212	3,332
Kecsemét	29 June	116	2,790	1 July	203	223	2,364
Kunhegyes to Szolnok	29 June	117	2,038	1 July	318	350	1,370
Debrecen	29 June	118	3,026	1 July	50	55	2,921

	Gaško List			Glaser List		This Analysis	
Resided at or transport from	Date Arr. Košice	Train No.	People arriving	Date Arr. Birkenau	Men selected	Women selected	People Killed
Left Sárvár 29 June	30 June	119	3,105	7 July	339	373	2,393
	5 July						
Szombathely	5 July	120	3,103	7 July	288	317	2,498
Kaposvár	6 July	121	3,050	7 July	219	241	2,590
Magyaregregy to Pecs	6 July	122	3,100	8 July	300	330	2,440
Kaposvár	6 July	123	2,066	8 July	209	230	1,627
Sopron	7 July	124	3,077	8 July	356	392	2,329
Pápa	7 July	125	2,793	8 July	361	397	2,035
Paks	7 July	126	1,072	8 July	335	371	366
Monor	7 July	127	3,549	9 July	259	285	3,005
Óbuda	7 July	128	3,151	9 July	193	212	2,746
Sárvár	7 July	129	2,204	9 July	220	242	1,742
Pecs	8 July	130	2,523	9 July	85	94	2,344
Óbuda	8 July	131	2,997	10 July	248	273	2,476
Monor	9 July	132	3,065	10 July	183	201	2,681
Óbuda	9 July	133	3,072	10 July	299	329	2,444
Budakalász	9 July	134	3,072	10 July	378	416	2,277
Monor	9 July	135	3,079	11 July	426	469	2,184
Duna-Bogdan to Bekésmegyer	9 July	136	1,924	11 July	409	450	1,065
	19 July	h	3,160	22 July	371	408	2,381
Rákoscsaba	20 July	137	1,230	22 July	11	12	1,207
(for Hung. Jews)	(146 trains)	i	3,160	25 July	2	2	3,156
				31 July	2	2	
From Hungary (Sárvár)	5 Aug		1,200	7 Aug.	344	378	478
From Slovakia			1,200	2 Sept.	6	7	1,187
From Slovakia			1,200	20 Sept.	31	34	1,135
From Budapest			1,200	20 Sept.	8	9	1,183

Im Lager Auschwitz eingetroffene Transporte:

16.V.	221	ung.	Juden
"	173	"	"
17.	247	"	"
"	14	pol.	"
18.	309	ung.	"
18.	441	ung.	"
18.	484	"	"
"	33	"	"
19.	581	"	"
"	468	"	"
"	507	"	"
20.	503	"	"
"	647	"	"
"	19	pol.	"
"	992	ung.	"
21.	412	"	"
21.	5	pol.	"
21.	127	ung.	"
21.	556	"	"
"	362	"	"
"	395	"	"
22.	487	"	"
"	368	"	"
"	471	"	"
"	575	"	"
23.	205	"	"
"	196	"	"
"	345	"	"
"	575	"	"
24.	499	"	"
"	630	"	"
24.	288	Russen	
"	494	ung.	"
"	470	"	"
25.	224	"	"
"	515	"	"
"	528	"	"
"	529	"	"
"	2	Zigeuner	
"	510	ung.	Juden
26.	551	ung.	"
26.	1	deutscher Jude	
"	485	ung.	Juden
"	674	"	"
"	509	"	"
"	500	"	"
27.	528	"	"
27.	606	"	"
"	520	"	"
"	635	"	"
"	441	"	"

28.V.	479	ung.	Juden
"	625	"	"
"	455	"	"
"	477	"	"
"	499	"	"
"	282	"	"
"	211	"	"
"	304	"	"
"	155	"	"
30.	506	"	"
"	170	"	"
"	457	"	"
"	554	"	"
31.	538	"	"
31.	592	"	"
"	2	Zigeuner	
"	466	ung.	Juden

Zusammen:	28.457
davon	292 Arier
Rest:	28.165 Juden

1.VI.	429	ung. Juden
1.	519	" "
"	426	" "
"	696	" "
"	165	" "
"	277	Russen
2.	620	ung. Juden
"	510	" "
"	379	" "
"	5	Zigeuner
"	419	ung. Juden
3.	576	" "
"	543	" "
"	497	" "
"	1	Zigeuner
"	286	ung. Juden
"	443	" "
"	363	" "
"	3	Italiener
"	358	ung. Juden
"	496	" "
5.	441	" "
"	404	" "
"	416	" "
"	397	" "
6.	441	" "
"	524	" "
"	401	" "
7.	376	" "
"	328	" "
"	269	" "
"	444	" "
8.	405	" "
"	138	" "
9.	280	" "
"	279	" "
10.	166	" "
"	5	Zigeuner
11.	329	ung. Juden
12.	3	" "
12.	5	" "
"	84	" "
13.	111	" "
13.	162	" "
"	59	" "
14.	208	" "
"	66	" "
"	389	" "
15.	172	" "
"	256	" "
"	62	" "
"	620	" "
16.	53	"
"	9	italienische Juden
"	12	deutsche Juden
"	355	ung. Juden

17.5.	195	ung. Juden
"	190	" "
"	5	Zigeuner
"	353	ung. Juden
"	207	" "
18.	405	" "
"	255	" "
26.	17	juedische Mischling
27.	215	ung. Juden
28.	2	jugoslav. Juden
"	6	deutsche Juden
"	232	ung. Juden
29	236	" "
"	206	" "
"	193	" "
"	12	poln. Juden
"	5	poln. Juden
"	203	ung. Juden
30.	509	griechische Juden
"	180	italienische Juden

Zusammen: 20.316
davon   296 Arier
Rest: 20.020 Juden

1.VII.	318	ung. Juden
"	50	" "
"	339	" "
"	6	Russen
"	2	deutsche Juden
"	1000	tschechische Juden
"	5	Italiener
4.	400	tschechische Juden
"	398	franzoesische Juden
6.	2	Zigeuner
7.	44	russische Kriegsgefangene
7.	288	ung. Juden
"	219	" "
8.	300	" "
"	209	" "
"	356	" "
"	361	" "
"	335	" "
9.	259	" "
"	193	" "
"	220	" "
"	85	" "
10.	248	" "
"	183	" "
"	125	tschechische Juden
"	299	ung. Juden
"	378	ung. Juden
11.	426	" "
"	409	" "
14.	10	deutsche Juden
"	2	italienische Juden
"	1	Zigeuner
19.	3	Zigeuner
"	9	poln. Juden
22.	371	ung. Juden
"	11	" "
"	8	Polen
"	34	Russen (K.G.)
23.	85	pol. Juden
25.	25	Polen
"	2	ung. Juden
26.	1	Zigeuner
28.	463	pol. Juden
"	376	Polen
"	21	russ. Kriegsgefangene
"	3	Z.Russen
29.	684	gemischter Transport
		(32 Franzosen, 182 Deutsche, 243 Polen. 227 Juden)
"	2	Zigeuner
30.	1,298	pol. Juden

31.VII.	26	Russen
"	2	ung. Juden
"	25	Polen
"	1.198	pol. Juden
zusammen:	12.443	
davon	739	Arier
Rest:	11.704	Juden

1.VIII.	1.616	Juden
"	129	pol. Juden (Kinder)
"	547	" "
3. "	6	it. Juden
"	10	diverse Juden
4. "	1.441	pol. Juden
"	109	russ. Kriegsgefangene
5. "	46	pol. Juden
"	1432	" "
"	9	franzoesische Juden
6. "	43	polnische Juden
"	129	" Juden
"	140	" "
7. "	114	" "
"	344	ung. Juden
"	23	polnische Juden
8. "	9	italienische Mischlinge
"	2	Zigeuner
"	80	italienische Juden
"	148	polnische Juden
9. "	288	" " aus Litzmannstadt
10. "	415	" " " "
11. "	16	" " " "
"	539	" " " "
"	440	" " " "
13. "	643	" " " "
14. "	1.859	" " " Warschau
15. "	473	" " " Litzmannstadt
16. "	496	" " " "
16. "	346	Griechische Juden aus Rhodos
17. "	8	kroatische Juden aus Litzmannstadt
"	412	polnische Juden aus Kattowitz
"	10	" " " Kattowitz
18. "	598	" " " Litzmannstadt
19. "	434	" " " "
20. "	522	" " " "
21. "	469	" " " "
22. "	688	" " " "
23. "	557	" " " "
24. "	477	" " " "
24. "	435	" " " "
25. "	598	" " " "
"	546	" " " "
26. "	748	" " " "
"	589	" " " "
27. "	788	" " " "
"	545	" " " "
28. "	630	" " " "
"	568	" " " "
29. "	265	" " " "
"	784	" " " "
30. "	483	" " " "
"	925	" " " "
31. "	184	" " " "
"	245	" " " "
"	28	" " " "
"	116	franzoesische Mischlinge aus Lyon

Zusammen: 24.174 davon 2.070 Arier   Rest: 22.104 Juden

Notes

Notes